THIS IS WOMEN'S WORK

An Anthology of Prose and Poetry

THIS IS WOMEN'S WORK

An Anthology of Prose and Poetry

Edited by Susan Efros
Graphics edited by Honor Johnson

Panjandrum Press   1974
San Francisco

First Printing: December, 1974
Second Printing: January, 1976

Library of Congress Cataloging in Publication Data

Efros, Susan, comp.
    This is women's work. ───────────────

    1. Women's writings, American.   I.   Johnson,
Honor, comp.   II.   Title.
PS508.W7E4   811'.5'408   74-19118

Some of these poems were previously published in the following magazines, to whom grateful acknowledgment is given:

1) Cheri Fein: "The Earliest Days" was published in *Southern Poetry Review.*

2) Nancy Willard: "The poet invites the moon" appeared in *19 masks for the naked poet* (Kayak).

3) Jan Zaleski: "In Answer to What He Said" appeared in *Bastard Angel* #1.

4) Marge Piercy: "The Consumer" and "Gracious Goodness" were first published in *4-Telling* (Crossing Press, 1971), 16/53 *New:* Canadian and American Poetry. "All Clear" appeared in *Sojourner.*

Panjandrum Press
99 Sanchez Street
San Francisco, California 94114

TABLE OF CONTENTS

GRAPHICS

Cover illustration by Karen Breschi.

CONTRIBUTORS

ALTA lives in San Lorenzo. She is the founder of Shameless Hussy Press. Her latest books are *Momma* published by Times Change Press, New York, and *Theme and Variation* published by Aldebaran Press, Berkeley, Calif.

LAURA BEAUSOLEIL lives in San Francisco. A collection of her poems, *Autograph,* was recently published by Gallimaufry Press, San Francisco.

RENA BLAUNER lives in Berkeley. She is an editor and contributor to the *Wild Iris* magazine, a new women's West Coast magazine.

SANDY BOUCHER lives in San Francisco. She has recently had a collection of her stories, *Assaults and Rituals,* published by Mama's Press.

DOROTHY ANN BROWN lives in Berkeley. She is completing a dissertation on the formal and esthetic consequences of feminism in Virginia Woolf's novels.

GRACE BUTCHER lives in Chardon, Ohio. She teaches English at Kent State. Her latest book is *Rumors of Ecstasy . . . Rumors of Death,* published by Ashland Poetry Press, Ohio.

SUSAN KENNEDY (CALHOUN) lives in San Francisco. Her short stories have been published in *Worksheet* and *Transfer.*

LYNDA EFROS is a writer living in Berkeley.

SUSAN EFROS lives in Berkeley. She is a poet and journalist. A collection of her poems, *Two-Way Streets,* has recently been published by Jungle Garden Press of Fairfax, Calif.

CHERI FEIN lives in New York City, "where she is working to make her life grow with her poems / her poems grow with her life."

KATHLEEN FRASER lives in San Francisco. Her latest collection of poems, entitled *What I Want,* is published by Harper and Row. Currently, she is teaching Creative Writing at S.F. State University.

HEIDI GITTERMAN is a poet living on the East Coast.

SUSAN GRIFFIN lives in Berkeley. Her play *Voices* has just been published by Feminist Press. She is writing a book on Women and Nature to be published by Harper and Row in 1976.

JANA HARRIS lives in the East Bay. She is an editor of *Poetry Flash* magazine. A collection of her poems, *Pin Money,* is to be published by Jungle Garden Press this year.

HONOR JOHNSON is a painter and poet living in Los Angeles.

THALIA KITRILAKIS lives in Berkeley. She is an editor and contributing poet to *Wild Iris* magazine.

FANCHON LEWIS lives in Berkeley. "She is now concentrating on consciousness contraction."

RACHEL LODEN is a poet living in Berkeley.

ADRIANNE MARCUS is a part-time instructor at the College of Marin. Her latest book, entitled *The Photojournalist: Mark and Leibovitz,* is published by T. Y. Crowell and Book-of-the-Month Club.

ROCHELLE NAMEROFF lives in Berkeley. A collection of her poems, *Body Prints,* is published by Ithaca House, N.Y. She is currently working on a Ph.D. at U.C. Berkeley.

TILLIE OLSEN, a San Franciscan most of her life, is the author of *Tell Me a Riddle* and *Yonnondio: From the Thirties.* Her origin, identification and life are primarily working class, and she is a longtime feminist and activist. "One Out of Twelve: Women Writers in Our Century," a talk given to the MLA in 1971 and reprinted in *College English,* November 1972, is a companion piece to "Silences," concentrating solely upon women.
"Minor, Not Major: Why?" was included with Rebecca Harding Davis's *Life in the Iron Mills* (Feminist Press).

MARGE PIERCY lives in Wellfleet, Mass. She has had several books of poems published, including *To Be of Use,* and most recently *Living in the Open,* published by Knopf. She also is the author of the novel *Small Changes,* published by Doubleday.

JEANNE SIROTKIN lives in San Francisco. Her current collection of poems is *An Unzipped Dress,* from Golden Mountain Press, S.F. She is a member of Parachute Salon.

JULIA VINOGRAD lives in Berkeley. She has several books of poems, including *The Berkeley Bead Game* and *Uniform Opinions,* both published by Cody's Books of Berkeley.

JULIA VOSE lives in San Francisco. Her Essay "Anne Sexton: What about it?" is published by Smoking Mirror Press, S.F. She is poet-in-residence at Mount Zion Hospital.

GRACE WADE lives in San Francisco. She writes both prose and poetry. Her short story "Passing" appears in the Fall, 1975 issue of *Big Moon* magazine.

RUTH WEISS is a poet, playwright, filmmaker and poetry coordinator living in San Francisco. She has run programs at the Intersection and the Old Spaghetti Factory. Her work appears in numerous magazines and anthologies. She is currently working with Conahan Press on a series of serigraphed poems.

NANCY WILLARD lives with her husband and son in Poughkeepsie, N.Y. She teaches at Vassar. Her most recent book of poems is *Carpenter of the Sun,* Liveright-Norton.

SYBIL WOOD is a poet living in San Francisco. She has been published in *Gypsy Table* magazine.

JAN ZALESKI lives in Palo Alto, Calif., and is currently teaching writing in nursing homes. She is writing a "journal" about her experiences there.

ALISON ZIER lives in Chico, Calif. She is a poet, housewife and Women's Studies student at CSUC.

THE TIME TO BE defensive about Women's work is over; volumes of poetry, fiction and non-fiction, paintings and sculpture, speak for themselves. The Women's movement is mature enough to use the most stringent criteria in evaluating its work, criteria that define good art work in any realm, at any time. By 'good work' is meant art that meets the tests of universality, meaningfulness, and absolute truth of emotional information. Whenever artistic standards are 'shifted' or 'lowered' for the purposes of faddism, sensationalism, mere profit, or so-called political reasons, contributing artists, as well as the general public, suffer; people are hungry for quality.

Publishing or displaying less than the best is demeaning to serious, developing women artists. Individual writers, regardless of gender, must not only demand the best from themselves, but must be each other's best critics. Those who edit, publish, and read women's work, must keep in mind that women are capable of reaching the highest levels of artistic endeavor, and must be encouraged to do so.

Women find it easy to be supportive of each other's work, and this sensitive tool should not be undermined. However, supportiveness must be coupled with honesty, and strict, professional criticism, if it is ultimately to benefit the artist, and the world of art. This is not to say that because all women are not female Shakespeares, they should cease writing. There are innumerable, valid reasons to write besides making profound contributions to the literary world. Personal journals, poems, stories and paintings can be important tools for self-expression and growth, without becoming artistic masterpieces or world-renowned successes.

Thus, to encourage all women to write is in harmony with demanding high quality. It is only to say that when the time comes to print voluminous copies of one's writing, the very standards we are speaking of must be employed. Not every word committed on the typewriter is worth running off on the press, just as not every completed painting should be hung in a gallery. This reality, however, should never diminish the value of creative expression, or the individual's prerogative to explore a craft, to aim for artistic perfection.

But in the final analysis, artists are obligated to publish the best, and anything less stunts individual, artistic development, and denies a readership or audience what it should expect and deserve, namely the highest quality attainable in every imaginable area of art.

Here is a potpourri of writers who happen to be women; some have been published before, some have not, but all have something to say to us. In editing this collection, I chose to select material on the basis of quality, not "popular women's topics." The unifying factor of this volume is that the work is good, meets high standards of art and transcends a world intensely overrun with cheap imitations and faddist, noisy stimulation.

Subject matter is not the point. The scope of any artist, at any time, is unlimited, and women as well as all other artists, maintain the internal freedom and choice to express what they as individuals are compelled to communicate. When internal process and high standards are not allowed to operate, when artists do not take themselves and the arts completely seriously, we cheat our culture of the best that people have to offer.

Not only is the time to be defensive long past, but now that women have begun to write, and are meeting high standards in their work, as well as learning to effectively criticize each other's work in an intelligent and sophisticated fashion, we are assured of an avalanche of new visions and perspectives from the female in the arts. This is not a time to justify one's purpose or right to create; it is a time to work, and to work diligently! And I am delighted to add, it is a time to celebrate the Woman artist who is coming into her own, and enriching her culture in the process.

Susan Efros
Berkeley, 1974

SILENCES*
When Writers Don't Write

L ITERARY HISTORY and the present are dark with silences: some the silences for years by our acknowledged great; some silences hidden; some the ceasing to publish after one work appears; some the never coming to book form at all.

What is it that happens with the creator, to the creative process in that time? What *are* creation's needs for full functioning? Without intention of or pretension to literary scholarship, I have had special need to learn all I could of this over the years, myself so nearly remaining mute and having let writing die over and over again in me.

These are not *natural* silences, what Keats called *agonie ennuyeuse* (the tedious agony), that necessary time for renewal, lying fallow, gestation, in the natural cycle of creation. The silences I speak of here are unnatural; the unnatural thwarting of what struggles to come into being, but cannot. In the old, the obvious parallels: when the seed strikes stone; the soil will not sustain; the spring is false; the time is drought or blight or infestation; the frost comes premature.

The very great have known such silences—Thomas Hardy, Melville, Rimbaud, Gerard Manley Hopkins. They tell us little as to why or how the creative working atrophied and died in them—if it ever did.

"Less and less shrink the visions then vast in me," writes Thomas Hardy in his thirty-year ceasing from novels after

---

*Part of a talk entitled "Death of the Creative Process" given at the Radcliffe Institute in 1963. Reprinted from *Harper's Magazine,* October, 1965. Copyright © 1965 by the author.

the Victorian vileness to his *Jude the Obscure*. ("So ended his prose contributions to literature, his experiences having killed all his interest in this form"—the official explanation.) But the great poetry he wrote to the end of his life was not sufficient to hold, to develop, the vast visions which for twenty-five years had had scope in novel after novel. People, situations, interrelationships, landscape—they cry for this larger life in poem after poem.

It was not visions shrinking with Hopkins, but a different torment. For seven years he kept his religious vow to refrain from writing poetry, but the poet's eye he could not shut, nor win "elected silence to beat upon [his] whorled ear." "I had *long* had haunting my ear the echo of a poem which now I realized on paper," he writes of the first poem permitted to end the seven years' silence. But poetry ("to hoard unheard; be heard, unheeded") could be only the least and last of his heavy priestly responsibilities. Nineteen poems were all he could produce in his last nine years—fullness to us, but torment pitched past grief to him, who felt himself become "time's eunuch, never to beget."

Silence surrounds Rimbaud's silence. Was there torment of the unwritten; haunting of rhythm, of visions; anguish at dying powers; the seventeen years after he abandoned the unendurable literary world? We know only that the need to write continued into his first years of vagabondage, and that on his deathbed he spoke again like a poet-visionary.

Melville's stages to his thirty-year prose silence are clearest. The presage is in his famous letter to Hawthorne, as he had to hurry *Moby Dick* to an end:

> I am so pulled hither and thither by circumstances. The calm, the coolness, the silent grass growing mood in which a man ought always to compose, that can seldom be mine. Dollars damn me. What I feel most moved to write, that is banned, it will not pay. Yet altogether, write the other way I cannot. So the result is a final hash.

Reiterated in *Pierre* (Melville himself), writing "that book whose unfathomable cravings drink his blood . . .

> when at last the idea obtruded that the wiser and profounder he should grow, the more he lessened his chances for bread.

To have to try final hash; to have one's work met by "drear ignoring"; to be damned by dollars into a Customs House job; to have only occasional weary evenings and Sundays left for writing—

> How bitterly did unreplying Pierre feel in his heart that to most of the great works of humanity, their authors had given not weeks and months, not years and years, but their wholly surrendered and dedicated lives.

Is it not understandable why Melville began to burn work, then refused to write it, "immolating" it, "sealing in a fate subdued"? Instead he turned to sporadic poetry, manageable in a time sense, "to nurse through night the ethereal spark" where once had been "flame on flame." A thirty-year night. He was nearly seventy before he could quit the Customs dock and again have full time for writing, start back to prose. "Age, dull tranquilizer," and devastation of "arid years that filed before" to work through before he could restore the creative process. Three years of tryings before he felt capable of beginning *Billy Budd* (the kernel waiting half a century); three years more, the slow, painful, never satisfied writing and rewriting of it.

Kin to these years-long silences are the *hidden* silences; work aborted, deferred, denied—hidden by the work which does come to fruition. Hopkins' last years rightfully belong here, as does Kafka's whole writing life, that of Mallarme, Olive Schreiner, probably Katherine Anne Porter, and many other contemporary writers.

Censorship silences. Deletions, omissions, abandonment of the medium (as with Thomas Hardy). Self-censorship, like Mark Twain's. Publishers' censorship, refusing subject matter or treatment. Religious, political censorship—sometimes spurring inventiveness—most often (read Dostoevski's letters) a wearing attrition.

The extreme of this: those writers physically silenced by governments. Isaac Babel, the years of imprisonment, what took place in him with what wanted to be written? Or in Oscar Wilde, who was not permitted even a pencil until the last months of his imprisonment?

Other silences. The truly memorable poem, story, or book, then the writer never heard from again. Was one work all the writer had in him, and he respected literature too much to repeat himself? Was there the kind of paralysis psychiatry might have helped? Were the conditions not present for establishing the habits of creativity (a young Colette who lacked a Willy to lock her in her room each day? or other claims, other responsibilities so writing could not be first)? It is an eloquent commentary that this one-book silence is true of most Negro writers; only eleven, these last hundred years, have published more than twice.

There is a prevalent silence I pass by quickly, the absence of creativity where it once had been; the ceasing to create literature, though the books keep coming out, year after year. That suicide of the creative process Hemingway describes so accurately in *The Snows of Kilimanjaro:*

> He had destroyed his talent himself—by not using it, by betrayals of himself and what he believed in, by drinking so much that he blunted the edge of his perceptions, by laziness, by sloth, by snobbery, by hook and by crook; selling vitality, trading it for security, for comfort.

No, not Scott Fitzgerald. His not a death of creativity, not silence, but what happens when (his words) there is "the sacrifice of talent, in pieces, to preserve its essential value."

Almost unnoted are the foreground silences, *before* the achievement. (Remember when Emerson hailed Whitman's genius, he guessed correctly, "which yet must have had a long *foreground* for such a start.") George Eliot, Joseph

4

Conrad, Isak Dinesen, Sherwood Anderson, Elizabeth Madox Roberts, Joyce Cary—all close to, or in, their forties before they became writers; Lampedusa, Maria Dermout (*The Ten Thousand Things*), Laura Ingalls Wilder, the "children's writer," in their sixties. Their capacities evident early in the "being one on whom nothing is lost." Not all struggling and anguished, like Anderson, the foreground years; some needing the immobilization of long illness or loss, or the sudden lifting of responsibility to make writing necessary, make writing possible; others waiting circumstances and encouragement (George Eliot, her Henry Lewes; Laura Wilder, a daughter's insistence that she transmute her storytelling gift onto paper).

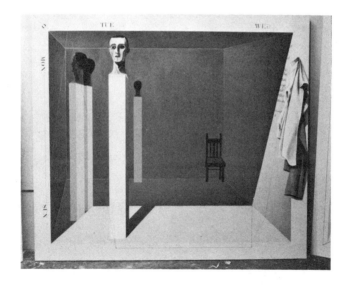

VERY CLOSE to this last grouping are the silences where
the lives never came to writing. Among these, the mute
inglorious Miltons: those whose waking hours are all
struggle for existence; the barely educated; the illiterate;
women. Their silence the silence of centuries as to how life
was, is, for most of humanity. Traces of their making, of
course, in folk song, lullaby, tales, language itself, jokes,
maxims, superstitions, but we know nothing of the creators
or how it was with them. In the fantasy of Shakespeare born
in deepest Africa (as at least one Shakespeare must have
been), was the ritual, the oral storytelling a fulfillment? Or
was there restlessness, indefinable yearning, a sense of re-
striction? Was it as Virginia Woolf in *A Room of One's Own*
guesses—about women?

> Genius of a sort must have existed among them, as
> it existed among the working classes, but certainly
> it never got itself onto paper. When, however, one
> reads of a woman possessed by devils, of a wise
> woman selling herbs, or even a remarkable man
> who had a remarkable mother, then I think we are
> on the track of a lost novelist, a suppressed poet,
> or some Emily Bronte who dashed her brains out
> on the moor, crazed with the torture her gift had
> put her to.

Rebecca Harding Davis whose work sleeps in the forgotten (herself as a woman of a century ago so close to remaining mute) also guessed about the silent in that time of
the twelve-hour-a-day, six-day work week. She writes of the
illiterate ironworker in "Life in the Iron Mills" who sculp-
tured great shapes in the slag, "his fierce thirst for beauty,
to know it, to create it, to *be* something other than he is—a
passion of pain," *Margaret Howth* in the textile mill:

> There were things in the world, that like herself,
> were marred, did not understand, were hungry to

know. . . . Her eyes quicker to see than ours, delicate or grand lines in the homeliest things. . . .
Everything she saw or touched, nearer, more
human than to you or me. These sights and sounds
did not come to her common; she never got used to
living as other people do.

She never got used to living as other people do. Was that
one of the ways it was?

So some of the silences, incomplete listing of the incomplete, where the need and capacity to create were of a high
order.

The Frightful Task

NOW, WHAT *is* the work of creation and the circumstances it demands for full functioning—as told in the
journals and notes of the practitioners themselves: Henry
James, Katherine Mansfield, Gide, Virginia Woolf; the letters of Flaubert, Rilke, Conrad; Thomas Wolfe's *Story of a
Novel*, Valery's *Course in Poetics*. What do they explain of
the silences?

"Constant toil is the law of art, as it is of life," says (and
demonstrated) Balzac:

To pass from conception to execution, to produce,
to bring the idea to birth, to raise the child labori-
ously from infancy, to put it nightly to sleep sur-
feited, to kiss it in the mornings with the hungry
heart of a mother, to clean it, to clothe it fifty times
over in new garments which it tears and casts
away, and yet not revolt against the trials of this
agitated life—this unwearying maternal love, this
habit of creation—this is execution and its toils.

"Without duties, almost without external communica-
tion," Rilke specifies, "unconfined solitude which takes

every day like a life, a spaciousness which puts not limit to vision and in the midst of which infinities surround."

Unconfined solitude as Joseph Conrad experienced it:

> For twenty months I wrestled with the Lord for my creation . . . mind and will and conscience engaged to the full, hour after hour, day after day . . . a lonely struggle in a great isolation from the world. I suppose I slept and ate the food put before me and talked connectedly on suitable occasions, but I was never aware of the even flow of daily life, made easy and noiseless for me by a silent, watchful, tireless affection.

So there is a homely underpinning for it all, the even flow of daily life made easy and noiseless.

"The terrible law of the artist"—says Henry James—"the law of fructification, of fertilization. The old, old lesson of the art of meditation. To woo combinations and inspirations into being by a depth and continuity of attention and meditation."

"That load, that weight, that gnawing conscience," writes Thomas Mann—

> That sea which to drink up, that frightful task. . . . The will, the discipline and self-control to shape a sentence or follow out a hard train of thought. From the first rhythmical urge of the inward creative force towards the material, towards casting in shape and form, from that to the thought, the image, the word, the line, what a struggle, what Gethsemane.

Does it become very clear what Melville's Pierre so bitterly remarked on, and what literary history bears out, why most of the great works of humanity have come from wholly surrendered and dedicated lives? How else sustain the constant toil, the frightful task, the terrible law, the continuity? Full self, this means, full time for the work. (That time for which Emily Dickinson withdrew from the world.)

But what if there is not that fullness of time, let alone

totality of self? What if the writer, as in some of these silences, must work regularly at something besides his own work—as do nearly all in the arts in the United States today?

I know the theory (kin to starving in the garret makes great art) that it is this very circumstance which feeds creativity. I know, too, that for the beginning young, for some who have such need, the job can be valuable access to life they would not otherwise know. A few (I think of the doctors, Chekhov and William Carlos Williams) for special reasons sometimes manage both. But the actuality testifies: substantial creative work demands time, and with rare exceptions only full-time workers have created it. Where the claims of creation cannot be primary, the results are atrophy; unfinished work; minor effort and accomplishment; silences. (Desperation which accounts for the mountains of applications to the foundations for grants—undivided time—in the strange breadline system we have worked out for our artists.)

Twenty years went by on the writing of *Ship of Fools,* while Katherine Anne Porter, who needed only two years, was "trying to get to that table, to that typewriter, away from my jobs of teaching and trooping this country and of keeping house." "Your subconscious needed that time to grow the layers of pearl," she was told. Perhaps, perhaps, but I doubt it. Subterranean forces can make you wait, but they are very finicky about the kind of waiting it has to be. Before they will feed the creator back, they must be fed, passionately fed, what needs to be worked on. "We hold up our desire as one places a magnet over a composite dust from which the particle of iron will suddenly jump up," says Paul Valery. A receptive waiting, that means, not demands which prevent "an undistracted center of being." And when the response comes availability to work must be immediate. If not used at once, all may vanish as a dream; worse, future creation be endangered, for only the removal and development of the material frees the forces for further work.

There is a life in which all this is documented: Franz Kafka's. For every one entry from his diaries here, there are fifty others which testify as unbearably to the driven stratagems for time, the work lost (to us), the damage to the creative powers (and the body) of having to deny, interrupt, postpone, put aside, let work die.

"I cannot devote myself completely to my writing," Kafka explains (in 1911). "I could not live by literature, if only, to begin with, because of the slow maturing of my work and its special character." So he worked as an official in a state insurance agency, and wrote when he could.

> These two can never be reconciled. . . . If I have written something one evening, I am afire the next day in the office and can bring nothing to completion. Outwardly I fulfill my office duties satisfactorily, not my inner duties however, and every unfulfilled inner duty becomes a misfortune that never leaves. What strength it will necessarily drain me of.

> [1911] No matter how little the time or how badly I write, I feel approaching the imminent possibility of great moments which could make me capable of anything. But my being does not have sufficient strength to hold this to the next writing time. During the day the visible world helps me; during the night it cuts me to pieces unhindered. . . . Calling forth such powers which are then not permitted to function.

Which are then not permitted to function.

> [1912] When I begin to write after such a long interval, I draw the words as if out of the empty air. If I capture one, then I have just this one alone, and all the toil must begin anew.

> [1914] Yesterday for the first time in months, an indisputable ability to do good work. And yet wrote only the first page. Again I realize that everything written down bit by bit rather than all at once in the course of the larger part is inferior,

and that the circumstances of my life condemn me to this inferiority.

[1915] My constant attempt by sleeping before dinner to make it possible to continue working [writing] late into the night, senseless. Then at one o'clock can no longer fall asleep at all, the next day at work insupportable, and so I destroy myself.

[1917] Distractedness, weak memory, stupidity. . . . Always this one principal anguish—if I had gone away in 1911 in full possession of all my powers. Not eaten by the strain of keeping down living forces.

Eaten into tuberculosis. By the time he won through to self and time for writing, his body could live no more. He was forty-one.

I think of Rilke who said: "If I have any responsibility, I mean and desire it to be responsibility for the deepest and innermost essence of the loved reality [writing] to which I am inseparably bound"; and who also said: "Anything alive, that makes demands, arouses in me an infinite capacity to give it its due, the consequences of which completely use me up." These were true with Kafka, too, yet how different their lives. When Rilke wrote that about responsibility, he is explaining why he will not take a job to support his wife and baby, nor live with them (years later will not come to his daughter's wedding nor permit a two-hour honeymoon visit lest it break his solitude where he awaits poetry). The "infinite capacity" is his explanation as to why he cannot even bear to have a dog. Extreme—and justified. He protected his creative powers.

KAFKA'S, Rilke's "infinite capacity" and all else that
has been said here of the needs of creation, illuminate
women's silence of centuries. I will not repeat what is in Virginia Woolf's *A Room of One's Own,* but talk of this last
century and a half in which women have begun to have voice
in literature. (It has been less than that time in Eastern
Europe, and not yet, in many parts of the world.)

In the last century, of the women whose achievements
endure for us in one way or another, nearly all never married (Jane Austen, Emily Brontë, Christina Rossetti, Emily
Dickinson, Louisa May Alcott, Sarah Orne Jewett) or married late in their thirties (George Eliot, Elizabeth Barrett
Browning, Charlotte Brontë, Olive Schreiner). I can think of
only three (George Sand, Harriet Beecher Stowe, and Helen
Hunt Jackson) who married and had children as young
women. All had servants.

In our century, until very recently, it has not been so dif-
ferent. Most did not marry (Lagerlöf, Cather, Glasgow,
Gertrude Stein, Sitwell, Gabriela Mistral, Elizabeth Madox
Roberts, Charlotte Mew, Welty, Marianne Moore) or, if
married, have been childless (Undset, Wharton, Woolf,
Katherine Mansfield, H. H. Richardson, Bowen, Dinesen,
Porter, Hellman, Dorothy Parker). Colette had one child. If I
include Kay Boyle, Pearl Buck, Dorothy Canfield Fisher,
that will make a small group who had more than one child.
Nearly all had household help.

Am I resaying the moldy theory that women have no
need, some say no capacity, to create art, because they can
create babies? And the additional proof is precisely that the
few women who have created it are nearly all childless? No.

The power and the need to create, over and beyond repro-
duction, is native in both men and women. Where the gifted
among women (*and men*) have remained mute, or have
never attained full capacity, it is because of circumstances,

inner or outer, which oppose the needs of creation.

Wholly surrendered and dedicated lives; time as needed for the work; totality of self. But women are traditionally trained to place others' needs first, to feel these needs as their own (the "infinite capacity"); their sphere, their satisfaction to be in making it possible for others to use their abilities. This is what Virginia Woolf meant when, already a writer of achievement, she wrote in her diary:

> Father's birthday. He would have been 96, 96, yes, today; and could have been 96, like other people one has known; but mercifully was not. His life would have entirely ended mine. What would have happened? No writing, no books;—inconceivable.

It took family deaths to free more than one woman writer into her own development. Emily Dickinson freed herself, denying all the duties expected of a woman of her social position except the closest family ones, and she was fortunate to have a sister, and servants, to share those. How much is revealed of what happened to their own talents in the diaries of those sisters of great men, Dorothy Wordsworth, Alice James.

And where there is no servant or relation to assume the responsibilities of daily living? Listen to Katherine Mansfield in the early days of her relationship with John Middleton Murry, when they both dreamed of becoming great writers:

> The house seems to take up so much time. . . . I mean when I have to clean up twice over or wash up extra unnecessary things, I get frightfully impatient and want to be working [writing]. So often this week you and Gordon have been talking while I washed dishes. Well someone's got to wash dishes and get food. Otherwise "there's nothing in the house but eggs to eat." And after you have gone I walk about with a mind full of ghosts of saucepans and primus stoves and "will there be enough to go around?" And you calling, whatever

I am doing, writing, "Tig, isn't there going to be tea? It's five o'clock."

I loathe myself today. This woman who superintends you and rushes about slamming doors and slopping water and shouts "You might at least empty the pail and wash out the tea leaves." O Jack, I wish that you would take me in your arms and kiss my hands and my face and every bit of me and say, "It's all right, you darling thing, I understand."

A long way from Conrad's favorable circumstance for creation: the flow of daily life made easy and noiseless.

And, if, in addition to the infinite capacity, to the daily responsibilities, there are children?

Balzac, you remember, described creation in terms of motherhood. Yes, in intelligent passionate motherhood there are similarities, and in more than the toil and patience. The calling upon total capacities; the re-living and new using of the past; the comprehensions; the fascination, absorption, intensity. All almost certain death to creation.

Not because the capacities to create no longer exist, or the need (though for a while, as in any fullness of life, the need may be obscured) but because the circumstances for sustained creation are almost impossible. The need cannot be first. It can have at best, only part self, part time. (Unless someone else does the nurturing. Read Dorothy Fisher's "Babushka Farnham" in *Fables for Parents.*) More than in any human relationship, overwhelmingly more, motherhood means being instantly interruptible, responsive, responsible. Children need one *now* (and remember, in our society, the family must often be the center for love and health the outside world is not). The very fact that these are needs of love, not duty, that one feels them as one's self; that there is no one else to be responsible for these needs, gives them primacy. It is distraction, not meditation, that becomes habitual; interruption, not continuity; spasmodic, not constant toil. The rest has been said here. Work interrupted, deferred, postponed, makes blockage—at best, lesser accomplishment. Unused capacities atrophy, cease to be.

When H. H. Richardson, who wrote the Australian classic *Ultima Thule*, was asked why she—whose children, like all her people, were so profoundly written—did not herself have children, she answered: "There are enough women to do the childbearing and childrearing. I know of none who can write my books." I remember thinking rebelliously, yes, and I know of none who can bear and rear my children either. But literary history is on her side. Almost no mothers —as almost no part-time, part-self persons—have created enduring literature—so far.

A Private Journey

IF I TALK NOW quickly of my own silences—almost presumptuous after what has been told here—it is that the individual experience may add.

In the twenty years I bore and reared my children, usually had to work on a job as well, the simplest circumstances for creation did not exist. Nevertheless writing, the hope of it, was "the air I breathed, so long as I shall breathe at all." In that hope, there was conscious storing, snatched reading, beginnings of writing, and always "the secret rootlets of reconnaissance."

When the youngest of our four was in school, the beginnings struggled toward endings. This was a time, in Kafka's words, "like a squirrel in a cage: bliss of movement, desperation about constriction, craziness of endurance."

Bliss of movement. A full extended family life; the world of my job (transcriber in a dairy-equipment company); and the writing, which I was somehow able to carry around within me through work, through home. Time on the bus, even when I had to stand, was enough; the stolen moments at work, enough; the deep night hours for as long as I could stay awake, after the kids were in bed, after the household tasks were done, sometimes during. It is no accident that the first work I considered publishable began: "I stand here ironing, and what you asked me moves tormented back and forth with the iron."

In such snatches of time I wrote what I did in those years, but there came a time when this triple life was no longer possible. The fifteen hours of daily realities became too much distraction for the writing. I lost craziness of endurance. What might have been, I don't know, but I asked for, and received, eight months' writing time. There was still full family life, all the household responsibilities, but I did not have to go out on a job. I had continuity, three full days, sometimes more, and it was in those months I made the mysterious turn and became a writing writer.

Then had to return to the world of work, someone else's work, nine hours, five days a week.

This was the time of festering and congestion. For a few months I was able to shield the writing with which I was so full against the demands of jobs on which I had to be competent, through the joys and responsibilities of family. For a few months. Always roused by the writing, always denied. "I could not go to write it down. It convulsed and died in me. I will pay." My work died. What demanded to be written, did not; it seethed, bubbled, clamored, peopled me. At last moved into the hours meant for sleeping. I worked now full time on temporary jobs, a Kelly, a Western Agency girl (girl!), wandering from office to office, always hoping we could manage two, three writing months ahead. Eventually there was time.

I had said: always roused by the writing, always denied. Now, like a woman made frigid, I had to learn response, to trust this possibility for fruition that had not been before. Any interruption dazed and silenced me. It took a long while of surrendering to what I was trying to write, of invoking Henry James' "passion, piety, patience," before I was able to re-establish work.

When again I had to leave the writing, I lost conscious-ness. A time of anesthesia. There was still an automatic noting that did not stop, but it was as if writing had never been. No fever, no congestion, no festering. I ceased being peopled, slept well and dreamlessly, took a "permanent" job. The few pieces which had been published seemed to have vanished like the not-yet-written. I wrote someone, unsent: "So long they fed each other—my life, the writing; the writing or hope of it, my life—and now they destroy each other." I knew, but did not feel the destruction.

A Ford grant in literature, awarded me on nomination by others, came almost too late. Time granted does not neces-sarily coincide with time that can be most fully used, as the congested time of fullness would have been. Still, it was two years.

To Give One's All

DROWNING IS NOT so pitiful as the attempt to rise, says Emily Dickinson. I do not agree, but I know of what she speaks. For a long time I was that emaciated survivor trem-bling on the beach, unable to rise and walk. Said differently, I could manage only the feeblest, shallowest growth on that devastated soil. Weeds, to be burnt like weeds, or used as compost. When the habits of creation were at last rewon, one book went to the publisher, and I dared to begin my present work. It became my center, engraved on it: "Evil is whatever distracts." (By now, had begun a cost to our family life, to my own participation in life as a human being.) I shall not tell the "rest, residue, and remainder" of what I was "leased, demised, and let unto" when once again I had to leave work at the flood to return to the Time Master, to business-ese and legalese. This most harmful of all my silences has ended, but I am not yet recovered, may still be a one-book instead of a hidden and foreground silence.

However that will be, perhaps we are in a time of more and more hidden and foreground silences, men *and* women. Denied full writing life, more may try to "nurse through night" (that part-time, part-self night) "the ethereal spark," but it seems to me there would almost have had to be "flame on flame" first, and time as needed afterwards, and enough of the self, the capacities, undamaged for the rebeginnings on the frightful task. I would like to believe this for what has not yet been written into literature. But it cannot reconcile for what is lost by unnatural silences.

ALL CLEAR

Loss is also clearance.
Emptiness is also receptivity.
No, I cannot pretend:
the cells of my body lack you
and keen their specific hunger.
Yet, a light slants over this bleak landscape
from the low yellow sun,
a burning kite caught in the branches.
There is a lightness in me, the absence
of the weight of your judgment
bearing on my nape,
the slow stain of your judgment
rusting the moment.
I go out with empty hands
and women touch me, lightly, while we talk.
The words, the problems, the sharp faces
jostle like winter birds at a feeding station
although the crumpled fields look deserted.
I like to walk in the cold gelid morning.

When it becomes clear I am not replacing you
don't think it is primarily
because you cannot be replaced.
Consider that I am taking pleasure
in space, visited but unoccupied
for every man I have loved
was like an army.

IMAGES EMERGING

In the closed box of the darkroom—
air tepidly stirred by an exhaust fan,
stained by a dull orange safelight—
I am printing a roll from our last time.

In the developer
from the refrigerator door of the paper
ghostly you emerge grinning.
Slowly as I rock the tray
you come at me, hands extended.
Each image surprises.
I'm poor at guessing expression, success
from negatives, so each eight by ten
dunked in the chemical
gives you to me, again,
a small miracle as your face
swims looking at me.

Have I stolen a slice of you?
fixed you here?
It is sensual, to stand brooding
in the bathwater pool of the darkroom
rocking the trays in small waves
till you magically coalesce.

But the union is false. I look
but you do not see me.
Paper under my fingertips,
scent of acetic acid.
You are rocked in a bed two hundred miles
from here and your dark is peopled
with other faces.

SEEDLINGS IN THE MAIL

Like mail order brides
they are lacking in glamor.
Drooping and frail and wispy,
they are orphaned waifs of some green catastrophe
from which only they have been blown to safety
swaddled in a few wraiths of sphagnum moss.
Windbreaks, orchards, forests of the mad
they huddle in the dirt
smaller than our cats.
The catalog said they would grow
to stand ninety feet tall.
I could plant them in the bathroom.
I could grow them in window pots,
twelve trees to an egg carton.
I could dig four into the pockets of my jeans.
I could wear some in my hair
or my armpits.
Ah, for people like us, followed
by forwarding addresses and dossiers and limping causes
it takes a crazy despairing faith
full of teeth as a jack o'lantern
to plant pine and fir and beech
for somebody else's grandchildren,
if there are any.

GRACIOUS GOODNESS

On the beach where we had been idly
telling the shell coins
cat's paw, cross-barred Venus, china cockle,
we both saw at once
the sea bird fall to the sand
and flap grotesquely.
He had taken a great barbed hook
out through the cheek and fixed
in the big wing.
He was pinned to himself to die,
a royal tern with a black crest blown back
as if he flew in his own private wind.
He felt good in my hands, not fragile
but muscular and glossy and strong,
the beak that could have split my hand
opening only to cry
as we yanked on the barbs.
We borrowed a clippers, cut and drew out the hook.
Then the royal tern took off, wavering,
lurched twice,
then acrobat returned to his element, dipped,
zoomed, and sailed out to dive for a fish.
Virtue: what a sunrise in the belly.
Why is there nothing
I have ever done with anybody
that seems to me so obviously right?

THE CONSUMER

My eyes catch and stick
As I wade in bellysoft heat.
Tree of miniature chocolates filled with liqueurs,
trees of earrings tinkling in the mink wind,
of Bach oratorios spinning light at 33⅓,
tree of Thailand silks murmuring changes.
Pluck, eat and grow heavy.
Choose and buy.
From each hair a wine bottle dangles.
A toaster is strung through my nose.
An elevator is installed in my spine.
The mouth of the empire
eats onward through the apple of all.
Armies of brown men
are roasting into coffee beans,
are melted into chocolate,
are pounded into copper.
Their blood is refined into oil,
black river oozing rainbows
of affluence.
Their bodies shrink
into grains of rice.
I have lost my knees.
I am the soft mouth of the caterpillar.
Men and landscapes are my food
and I grow fat and blind.

Your elephant adolescence in sandlots Brooklyn:
it sloshes like a washtub with nostalgia.
Heroes stalked in your attic dragging chains of words.
In the coalbin you lifted weights
your belly pink as strawberry icecream.
You counted your body hairs like daisies
foretelling love / notlove / notlove.
Pillows of snow, girls melted leaving damp rings.
At night you turned into a toad big as a gas storage tank
and brooded over Flatbush muttering warts
and curses imitated from your favorite books.
You lay in bed becoming snotgreen Dedalus:
you would not wash
wanting your Jewish mother to threaten you with rosaries,
excommunication, the hierarchic ashes of creaky saints.
In bed you were secretly thin with scorn
while your parents doted and fed you stuffed cabbage
and outside the frowsy neighbors
eating their newspapers like grass and growing mad
with the cold dim light of television flickering in their eyes
danced, danced in the streets
for the burning to death
of Julius and Ethel Rosenberg.

MOTHER

moth'er, n. (prob. after *mother* parent. fr. MD *modder* filth, mud.) A slimy membrane composed of yeast cells and bacteria which develops on the surface of alcoholic liquids undergoing acetous fermentation. It is added to wine or cider to produce vinegar.

—*Webster's New Collegiate Dictionary*

Unto the woman he said, I will greatly multiply thy sorrow and thy conception; in sorrow thou shalt bring forth children; and thy desire shall be to thy husband, and he shall rule over thee.

—*Genesis* 3:16

one)

I find no edge to this mourning.
But where the sea bears its ghost brides
white-veiled upon the land
all night my breast rips
against the gnarled rope of its mooring.

two)

Meat remembers. And I have pushed my pain
down the long halls like the janitor's broom.

The striae of my belly silver as abalone.
I turn over in my sleep and these two pink kittens
follow me, my tits.

three)

I don't know where to find a vase
for these beautiful roses. I am only a housewife
and upstairs someone is being swallowed.

four)

The castle is sprinkled with sleeping powder.
Pricking her finger
on the wicked witch's wheel, the princess waits
in thraldom for a kiss.
—Mother, I'm scared. The children here
are all mad. They play a bad game.
They say you are a slimy mucus membrane
and that Daddy sleeps covered with dried come.
I am awake.
It is only the pill inside of me that is sleeping.

five)

the hat-check girl in white tie and tails.
She smiles, and tiny lines
crack open on his face like fissures.

I leave the way I came, Mother
                                (by the door)
I hear my heart beating in my cunt
a clitoral drumming

am I my brother's keeper?
In the bowels of this house
the mad children scream and beat their spoons.

—As your father, it is my right
to lock you in her womb. —
Father, your key is soft. It's melting.

In the grass where we might run
an enemy army is encamping.
Men pound stakes into their own hands.
there is no end to their occupation.

six)

What are you doing
with your red eyes, your bulging belly,
and your borrowed rib?

Dig your birth-bed deep.

The bow of your spine is arching,
the string of your belly is taut.

They want to know if you are a slot machine,
and if they have hit the jackpot.

Tell them, Mother,
that your eyes are as red as the warrior,
and your arrows aimed for the heart.

WHAT THE SIRENS SANG

We repeat the same choices until the day we die,
because we keep on repeating the same internal
talk   until   the   day   we   die.
—Don Juan

This useless lace stitched around my moon blue sleeve.
Are these dunes?
I believe I hear sand
struggling in the maw of the wind,
whistling around her teeth like song.
Throwing back my quilt I stand
legs spread firm apart on Diablo's sweet summit
grinning like the eunuch god's favorite angel,
in torn T-shirt
thumbs stuck in my jeans pockets.

One wedding dress in white eyelet, dyed a deep red.
One maidenhead grown over like a grave.
Broken like a wishbone
of which I got the short end.
I am not enough.
The doctor prescribes me a cock.

At seven I floated beyond their reach,
beyond the raft where the suited men & girls laughed,
out on the looking glass lake
where the scented reeds are always further,
the lily pads startled by frogs that have just jumped.
I could have died
there, but I didn't.
I came back,
to Lucky Strike,

to tuna fish with mayonnaise on white,
to my mother's search for one honest sperm.
Back East, Daddy rode the waves.
Way out I lost his bobbing head.
When I found him again, he was smiling, cigar
cocked from his mouth, still lit.

At night the sea comes back to rock me.
A wave of arms & legs rolls over me
then melts into a jelly soup.
I am jelly all over.
Jelly plugs my cunt.
I stand poised above my life like a diver.
I hear my voice speaking to me from the deep water.
My hand, red-clawed as in the commercial,
reaches for a male hand.
But what man wants to hold hands with a lobster?
Indeed. Mine is withdrawn.

I rip the lace edgings off my sleeve,
rip my moon blue gown down its seams.
If you rescued me now, I would look like this:
naked, crazy as the Nullarbor-Nymph,
happier in the company of two kangaroos. .
But you do not rescue me.
& I do not wish to be rescued.

I come to the edge of the world of men.
A flat world.
I am afraid to fall asleep in that world,
to be caressed all night by reasonable monsters.
The sirens of the sand sing lullabies.
My deaf ears drop off like blossoms.
Behind them, pink buds are opening to a music of the
                                                        atoms.

A hawk shrieks, circling the room,

its grief encased in muscular wings.
The chordless voice rasps:
"You can't scream here like that!"
His hands twitch round my neck.
I let out a long scream which slits him neatly open.
Inside his belly
I pluck the shining apple of his power,
fed him bite by bite when I was born.

'WHEN YOU BECOME THAT
COLD SULLEN CREATURE MAN'

I have lived with that forbidding rigidness of limbs,
the colorless dead-set eyes, too many times
to want that veiled threat hanging like a dead hand's
weight upon this house. Only a scream
can crack that moon-like silence. No
human foot has ever walked there
save to plant a flag in the belly of its mother.
I give it no chance of survival. It is too dry
to weep, too tight to bleed, too timid
to go out of control & let the holy madness heal.
That thing dies off. Even now it prunes back,
prunes back its silence until only a bitter twig is left.
& its root is so tenuous, so cracked with doubt,
its sapless body splinters onto the outraged earth.

THE EXPERIMENT

A bony foot
Attached to three red sticks of
Dynamite by
Two arcs of tweedy rope
The kind that itches
Cuts the skin black
Tape attaching
Potential explosion
To automatic timer
The timer being the source
Of the horse's gasping
How can it swallow
Round metal falling in
And out of its throat
The low sound of little
Crackings
Straining jaw muscles snapping
Like popcorn
In an experiment
There are no mistakes
Only the eyes
Two bulges filling out
Like beach balls
How they would bounce
Now they seize
The small yard
The world

The animal
Man
Who forced it open
Its mouth
Like he forced his body to ride
Upon its back
For some reason
It does not understand the man
Is laughing
See
The horse
Its mouth torn open
Held wide
With a crow bar
And the foot inside
Could anything be more marvelous
Blood red
Bony
Metal bar eating through its gums
Up through its nose
Think of hot coals
Held in the pit
Of your arm
Toe nail scraping
Its cheek
Bits of horse meat
Bone and hair and hoof and foot
Blown high over the yard
Sky red
Over the man
Who is laughing
For some reason he does not understand
His wife
Is galloping towards him
Her four limbs pounding
The field
Her mouth thrown wide

Screeching
Her eyes seizing
The small yard
The world
The animal
Man
Who forced her open
For some reason they do not understand
The horse is dead
The small yard is red
A foot has disappeared
That of his wife
See
Could anything be more marvelous

POEM FOR MY FATHER

It has not rained
And shall not rain.
The air is dry and the earth
Is hard and cracked.

I am sitting in the garden
Naked,
Talking to my cat.

I tell him that I miss you,
Dear father,
As these flowers miss the rain.
And to bear the pain
I press a piece of broken glass
In each palm.

I see the blood
Drip onto the ground and
Slide into the cracks.
My heart is as dry and
Thirsty as this earth.

Tomorrow I shall be reasonable.
Dressed in mourning
I shall kiss your photograph
And put it away.

Today I cry for you
And shall not eat.
Nor shall the flowers drink.

To hold you again,
Dear father!
I should gladly water all the garden
With my blood.

INVOCATION

"Love, if you love me,
   lie next to me.
Be for me, like rain,
the getting out"
                        Robert Creeley

at night,
in the day, in the
day's dream ·

you never
appear you
reappear

the husk of your
past wrapped
in eyes that
slide & glitter
unaware of their
terror &
hard power

with eye ropes you
hold me
unarmed

taut, distanced
I want

to believe that it ties
on both ends
if my neck is
involved

it is a
dream, it's a
nightmarish love
all my own
& like a dream grows a
covering of the skin
a night wound when
touched by the day

it is
something
of a sleeper

there is only
A skin between
I put it there &
it was put
there, there
it's been said but
who can say
it was not meant to be
loosened

EUCALYPTUS GRAVE

I walk with you in the woods
as I walked in my dream
with rags
for the wounded hills

my language to mother the world
like screams, stoking
the pain in the trees
which breed
brood on my memory's fire

the stove
where I bridge burned my life
and kindle my fantasy
must bury it over

laying my hands
in the clear
wind
to loosen
the tangle of my mind
I anticipate
health
"the touch that could calm the wild waters"
and stretch out
those whirlpools of sensual days
burnt fast

the future
which enters the watery matrix
like steam
enters my life
I have to cross over

the mist
the lost past family fantasy
covered, recovered
like chairs
chained to trees

to rock
out this solitude of words
my burning
which cradles the sun

THE WELCOME

much like
the heat of a leaf

the range of
caring
extends all over
the trees, books, the
speaker in my window, in my
chest
is home
to me & to me

MACHINE

"anxiety is just another form of entertainment"
Frank O'Hara

it is all so thoroughly
predictable   say no
all a routine, oral
distemper no meaning
all a   burning head
hole bored through
tongue for essential
blasphemy the taking of
revenge in the eyes
of the poem

the poem: how
to get out
of my corner how to
get out

the toes are
encrusted, the feet
will not move
how to draw the lines & break
them   why the
couple on the bed
downstairs
I listen
avidly   monaural
exercise

easy to
speak in alien
rhythms

                    say yr name
          in code
lying on a codpiece
worn out
frightened for lines I go

     tail between my legs symbolic of
yr tongue between my legs
     symbolic of
nothing between anybody's legs
nothing between anybody

          exception:
          the words   /   take up time
      back to the mouth again
circular animals

THE SONG OF THE WOMAN
WITH HER PARTS COMING OUT

I am bleeding
the blood seeps in red
circles on the white
white of my sheet,
my vagina
is opening, opening
closing and opening;
wet, wet,
my nipples turn rose and hard
my breasts swell against my arms
my arms float out
like anemones
my feet slide on the wooden
floor,
dancing, they are dancing, I sing,
my tongue slips from my mouth
and my mind
imagines a
clitoris
I am the woman
I am the woman
with her parts coming out
with her parts coming out.

The song of the woman with
the top of her head ripping off, with
the top of her head ripping off
and she flies out

and she flies out
and her flesh flies out
and her nose rubs against her ass,
and her eyes love ass
and her cunt
swells and sucks and waves,
and the words spring from her mind
like fourth of July rockets,
and the words too come out,
lesbian, lesbian, lesbian, pee, pee, pee, pee, cunt, vagina,
dyke, sex, sex, sex, sex, sweat, tongue, lick, suck, sweet,
sweet, sweet, suck
and the other words march out too,
the words,
P's and Q's
the word
nice
the word
virginity,
the word
mother,
mother goodness mother nice good goodness good good should
should be good be mother be nice good
the word
pure
the word
lascivious
the word
modest
the word
no
the word
no
the word
no
and the woman
the woman

the woman
with her
parts coming out
never stopped
never stopped
even to
say yes,
but only
flew with
her words
with her words
with her words
with her parts
with her parts
coming
with her parts
        coming
        coming
        coming
        out.

THIS IS A STORY about two women who love each other. The beginning of the story is not just one beginning but two. Two women were born. They were born and lived each for twenty-eight years before they met, one wearing a beautiful pee-coat, the other in a white neck brace. Or rather, one writing poetry and reading it to everyone, the other writing poetry and folding it into a small square and putting it in her pocket. You could say that the one thought she loved the other more than the other loved her. Or rather that the other loved also a man and was not sure who she loved more, or rather who she wanted to be with. Or rather you could say that they loved each other equally, but one, or rather, both, did not believe the love was there. Or rather the one thought she was needed and so she served and believed that was why the other spoke of love. Or you could even say she never believed anyone loved her. And that might have been said about the other too, only she did know, because she felt happy at times, that there was love between the two. The question with her was more that she wanted all the love because she thought if the other gave away too much love in other places to other people there would not be enough left. And really, what she was sure she knew was that if the other ever got far enough away to love someone else she most certainly would prefer that other person, and then, she would go away. Well, any way, in the midst of all this fear of the one and the indecision of the other, they became twenty-nine and then they became thirty and they still lived in the same house and they still loved each other but they did not make love. That is they did not touch each other on the breasts or the vagina but only slept near one another or curled up together or stroked their heads, or rubbed their backs, or held one another, or kissed goodbye and in the morning. These things they did but it was what they did not do that made the one upset. Upset and angry and hurt and all those feelings. And the other felt bad, bad for causing the hurt, and the other felt anyway that she was always causing hurt, just by existing, or by sitting down and putting her feet on the ottoman. For instance, the one who wore the beautiful pee-coat and stuffed her poems in her pocket and did not want to make love would always take care of the other. The other was sick for a long while. And for instance, the caring one would say, to give an example which is very exaggerated but shows the point, "I am sorry that I cannot carry you up the stairs." And at first the other was very touched that the one would even want to carry her up the stairs but she said, "First, I am too heavy for you, and second, I can walk up the stairs myself." And this went on, this very conversation, for a while. But gradually the conversation changed and it became like this, "Really, I can't carry you up the stairs, I'm so tired." And then the other would say, "I never asked you to." And finally the one who didn't ask began to believe she had asked and decided she had to prove that she had offered to carry the other up the stairs, or at least would if she could, only everyone knew she had a weak back. And there were other conversations of a different and of the same nature. And both women worked very hard to show that each was good herself, and each woman felt each herself that she herself was very selfish. But there was a truth apart from the feelings and that was that the woman with the pee-coat, though she did not carry the talkative poet up the stairs, did nearly every thing else for her. And all the other could do was to say thank you or occasionally to loan the caring woman money. This she herself felt was very cheap since she knew there was no reason but luck that she had the money to loan or to give. But the caring woman felt guilty about the money. And in any case it was true that there is no comparison between money and caring. And the one who had been sick felt guilty. And so, she tried to give love. And this was only partly accepted, not in the sense of making love, but in the sense of belief. And in addition, the sick woman could not really accept the caring woman's care. She would at first pretend she did not need the care, and then if she asked for the care, did so in a tone of voice implying that the caring woman did not want to give care. You can see that nothing in this story is simple. You can see that but you must also begin to be suspecting the outcome. More and more, as the sickness and the caring went on, the two women felt selfish inside. Finally, they gave each other as much pain as they did love. And the one who wore the neck brace would say to the caring one, "You should feel guilty," and then later she would say, "Last night I was sick and you did not know," And she would also say, "I think you should not make love to me if you do not want to but I think you should make love to me." And she would also say, "You should not always do what you should but do what you want." As you can see the one was very confused. And the other, for her part, would say, "You should not be afraid that I will leave you because if you keep on acting afraid, I will leave you." And the other would also say, "You are always acting so fair; you are always acting so self-righteous." But if the one became then unfair, or angry, or even nasty, the other would say, "You'll be sorry," and she would walk out the door. This went on and on in between what the one still remembers as tenderness and love and joy until one night the conversation repeated itself again and the one with the folded up poems left the house again. And she did not come back. And the truth is that she may never have come back because the truth is that she wanted to die. And by this, the other was frightened almost to death. And this then is the ending of one story about the two and also the beginning of two more stories, as only time will tell.

To Reana and Susie

THERE WAS A woman who wrote about a freak who was made of swiss cheese with most of her parts missing. There was another writer who wrote about a woman with her parts coming out. This is about their friend who was a football.

This woman loved being a football, or she thought she loved being a football, or maybe, as is true with most feelings that older women have, as opposed to younger women who have purer feelings, she both loved and hated being a football.

When she loved it, she thought mainly of what she had done wrong to make the real person kick her. When she hated it, she huffed and puffed and rolled out of the kick's way. When she loved it, she understood why the person had to kick her, when she hated it, she found a voice and screamed, "Leave me alone, I hurt!" When she loved it, she'd roll right in front of a foot and smile winningly, when she hated it, she hid under anything and shut her face.

Sometimes she got very tired loving and hating so much, so often. She also got mixed up, she didn't know when to roll, scream, hide, huff, smile, understand. But the kickers were good and they never got mixed up about her. Oh, sure, they got mixed up about other things, but they knew she was there always waiting whether in love or hate, always waiting. Trained by over forty years of womanhood, trained by her mother, trained by her father, trained by her teachers, trained by her bosses, trained by her children, trained by her husband, trained by her friends, and bestest of all trained by the U. S. of A. that had trained them all, but surest of all trained by herself.

Her swiss cheese friend and coming out parts friend were trained too and often the three used words to share their love and hate. Then some of the parts would come back to all of them and the football woman would almost become a foot *and* a ball, instead of only a football, and the swiss cheese woman would almost become a solid cheese woman, and the coming out parts woman would almost get all her parts back. Even now, this minute, they get better and worse.

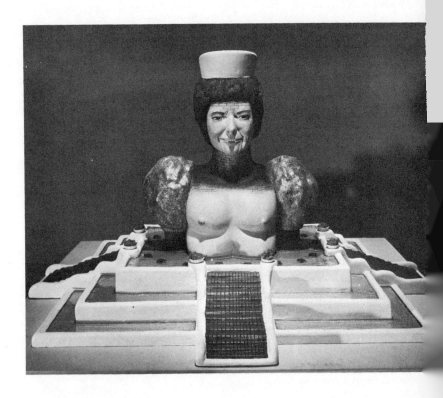

The Woman Who Was Angry

ONCE THERE WAS a woman who was angry all the time. She was angry at her husband. She was angry at children. She was even angry at the dog. And of course she was most angry at herself for being such an angry person.

It seemed that everyone was always getting in her way, taking away her time. She became obsessed with time. She began reading the obituary pages and counting how many years she might have left. She became desperate and miserly about her time, trying impossibly to hoard it.

The woman saw time everywhere, in slices of plastic-wrapped American cheese, time to be sandwiched between nursery school carpools and errands. Slices of pizza became slices of her life, her time, to be served to her family. And she had an image of a large hourglass whose sands were the days of her life. Mostly they slipped from the future through the present into the past so quickly she missed them entirely. Or if she was lucky enough to catch one grain and flow with it through the present, she was so angry that she had only the one grain that she could not enjoy it.

She did not like being angry. She could even remember days, weeks, years when she had not been so filled with anger. Maybe, she thought, there is a cure for my anger.

So the woman went to an anger specialist. He said that the treatment of such an extreme case as hers required that she visit him three times a week. It angered her that she must give away even more of her time, but she agreed. He invited her to lie down and tell him about her mother and her father, her dreams and her past. It seemed to the woman that he was interested in everything but her self, her time. Not wanting to offend, she said nothing and became an even angrier person.

One morning the woman was sitting at the kitchen table, so weighted with anger she could not move. And there were still lunches to be made. As she sat, wondering if she would ever find the strength to move again, the anger within her began to simmer and then boil with such force that it blew the top of her head open and 36 people climbed out. There was one for each year of time she had lived.

One left immediately for the beach to sit all day like a barnacle upon a rock. Another went upstairs for a nap. One packed an elegant lunch for her daughter and one read a story to her son. One sat down to write a poem, another to finish a weaving. One soaked in a hot tub and read a book. Another poured more coffee for her husband and asked about his day. One went for a walk in the woods with an old friend. One sat by the telephone. Another caught up on errands. One picked flowers in the garden. And one sat by her grandmother's grave and wept.

The woman realized, sitting there with the top of her head blown open, that no one was shouting or seething or bitching. Everyone was busy just living.

As if by prearranged signal, at the sound of the car horn, 35 of the 36 people climbed back into her head and the top banged shut. She knew it would never open again. The one who had gone to the beach turned into a barnacle and lived forever on that rock, nurtured by the sea and enveloped by a soft mist.

The woman went outside and put her children in the car that would take them to nursery school. She came back in and carefully tidied up the kitchen. Then she went upstairs, got into bed, curled up in the quilt she had pieced and died.

June, 1973

The Swiss Cheese Lady

STEP RIGHT UP ladies and gentlemen. Step right up to the greatest freak show on earth. Step right up and see the newest member of our freak family. Ladies and gentlemen, step right up and see the one and only—the Swiss Cheese Lady.''

A woman appears in front of the tattered purple curtain. There is a hole where once her heart was. There is a hole where once her sex was. There is a hole where once her mind was. She stands naked, illuminated from behind by pink and green lights that shine garishly through the holes in her body. She stands unseeing, immobile. Then she turns slowly so that all may see that the holes go through her body, that she is a genuine freak.

Encouraged by the barker, some of the crowd step forward to touch for themselves, to poke their fingers and hands through the holes where once her heart and sex and mind were. Some touch her hair and breasts too, as if sexually attracted by this strange creature who has holes where once her heart and sex and mind were. The woman stands unseeing, immobile.

When the crowd is finished with her, the Swiss Cheese Lady is led away by two very young women who wear pink and green leotards, theatrical eye make-up and bright painted fingernails. They slip an old cotton kimono over the woman's arms and lead her to a trailer. They seat her in an overstuffed chair, turn on the TV and leave, locking the door behind them. The woman sits unseeing, immobile, while from the screen the world blares messages about shampoos and tonics and sprays that will save her from fading beauty and age and lovelessness.

September, 1973

you, in yr levi jacket,
standing in the hall,
the lincs in yr face—

i am so lonely w/o you.
it is my pride that
keeps me away.
my pride
& yr fear.

i determine to be happy.
i meet the others; we
drink & laugh. & the hole
in my side is where yr
hand once touched me.
part of me is always
yours, ready,
always, to be at least
your friend.
i look for you on
every street. & the hole
in my side wants to
be ignored. to wait out
its loneliness.
just like a woman.

i nearly called you today.
idly wondering if i
remember yr number.
idly reflecting i could
no sooner forget my name.
part of me there is

that loves you.

(didn't we dance love)

& i have never
kissed yr lips.
do i dream of that.
do i remember my name.

stars whirling thru space.
there exists more
than me & my need.
i am sure of it.
just look at that star—
just look at that star—
(what if, right now, yr
 hand were there, just
 above the curve of
 my hip
& the blood rushing
in my ears
what have stars to do
w/ my universe

i must expand my horizons.
there is more than me & you.
there is the space between us.

SUSIE

susie was assigned to die.
she was assigned the faith of a devout catholic,
to marry a man who wanted her sister,
to bear children that died,
to be epileptic & unemployable,
what would a revolution have to do
to make susie happy?

we would rather lie alone
next to some man who pays the rent
than fight for survival in a
cockroached apartment where we
nightly fear rape, better the men
who dont want us any more
(their heads filled with fold outs?)
than a hand over our mouths
in the dark.

i clutch my pen, & i kno
i have sold out, & i pray
writing about it will
redeem me.

DESERT JOURNAL

Second Day

one has to throw it all away
notes — numbers
all the references
even the reverence of nothing
mirror — memory
all hinges swinging doors to possibility
even heat — cold
the backs of strangers
even cold — heat
the front familiar
even evil sweet

there is a point
where the last rescue
of love is possible
there is that point of lasting
the tall love calls
a cat shadow
on a wall
and is it a or the
or is it singularly plural?
who are you to say
how s should be placed
if?

THERE IS NO EVIL
ONLY RESTLESSNESS!

sometimes
someone
quite blond
and black
speaks out
like smoke
spoke without
knowing words
speaks out

the wheel of words
are left to the rule of the city
she will play
because
just because
no cause
no justice
not even how

but to know
is never to reap

to love is a yes
is a kind —
is not kind
is low
and someone will leap in
no year

the girl who doesn't drink
the girl who doesn't think
is the girl who
once
is was once

yes!

who are you to say
a or the?

Sixteenth Day

one could be so close
after all the dark spells
sent upon one
spent
dispelled —
after all the hell-bent hopes
bent to unfamiliar
after all
it is only how
not why or when
it is then
that it could be so close

oh the gypsy woman
oh the gypsy woman comes
sing the chorus of children free
as they watch her
as they watch me
from their opening
steps gleaming
as they watch her
as they watch me
mount the steps
from the abyss

bright things
rings the canyon

bright things
rings on fingers
desert-wings struck still

is it stone?
is it bone?
is it a throne for bird or beast?
does the sun rise in the east?
at least there is no chart
for the heart to set its at to

once upon
a nun on words
went wings
canyon-rings
to reach the human screech
the boundless of the beast
the soundless four-foot tone
known as coyote

coyote
liar
teller of all truths
tooth in check
beckons
to his other self
left loose & toothless
by coyote

once upon
a nun on words
crossed convent border
line & dot
to set the heart
where it's at upon

once upon

one could be so close
after all the dark spells
and hell-bent hopes
slope to the east
sent to the sun

what is this?
another game?

i would like
to make a call
to no-place!

Mornings
I'm pressed to elevators
Turning into tongues
Licking my mind
Always the spectre
Of sharks
Awaiting
The slightest movement
Any human reaction
Brings them all
To uncomfortable distance
Always the people tearing

we pay good wages for you to sit here plugged in
to our computer and have your brain vacuumed
fresh daily
to have your ear raped by countless profanities
of the corporate interest
if you want to feel   do it on your own time

I show them all by taking
A history of the Peloponnesian War
Into the toilet
There I shall take a stand

don't you know   you can only shit   on your own time

(What I glean from these sterile fields
Returning home

THE CIVIL SERVANT IS EATEN TOO

I entered the marble hall
Stumbling over missing arms and legs
Crawling on the walls
Toward the room carefully numbered A
ROOM WITH A VIEW
Nearwhich a large crowd had gathered
(Inside the half-witted were exchanging eyes
                                    with the blind
I rode a Gorgon's head to the counter-clerk
Who promptly bit off my left arm
Which was more than he had bargained for
As it was still loaded
With a pen
I scribbled obscenities on his liver
His head cracked open releasing a vaporous stream
Which carried us off laughing
Until we split along our seams
Miraculously
Our intestines aligned to form
A road in

PICNIC

As we slip   along the stair way
mounting the garden
oftentimes
it comes to pass
the bread   does not slice evenly
our tempers are ruffled
into lovely quilted gowns
for our errors and deceits.

On Sun days
it becomes necessary
to peel uncooked eggs
and roll membraneous gestures of friendship
into delicate containers.
a woman with a crystal face appears   and offers chicken soup
she has not heard of ethical suicide.
we are given a box of guilt and told not to open it
on penalty of expulsion   from the universe.
the intellectually curious pry open the coffin:

Rotting remains of a tortured asian child
sewn neatly into a black rag doll
float onto our table.

Thank You for Our Daily Bread
bury our words in words
bury our deeds in the garden
bury our children living

take time to escape the secret service men
who stick their victims
with sterilized bamboo picks.

IMAGES

They will come—
        posterity—
and analyze:
        my willow tree,
        my hair and breasts,
        my golden everythings.

And I will watch from Death
        (it is only a place,
        a slight barrier
        in the same way that hours
        have made Time what it is)—

and I will watch,
amused while they ponder
        my tangible air,
        my frequent "O,"
        my legs always running.

Being a dead poet
is not a bad deal.

Things are more relaxed here;
I do not revise.

MY NAME IN LIGHTS

One should always practice
going mad first:
the only and final performance
is opening night.

The body is stubborn
and needs to be rehearsed.
(The head is much more sensible.)
There are many setbacks:

The body thrashes, cracks,
in shock therapy
of violent weeping.
This must stop.

The spasmed hands
must be made to drop
the pen. (One could kill
with such a sharp point.)

Lines must be forgotten until
any word will do for screaming.
The eyes must see only
blink/blink of black neon.

Now, if it should be spring,
there is this to consider:
there will be no audience,
and no other actors.

This is the off-season for madness.
It takes a Great Desire

to succeed in this
empty theater. Or luck.

The only trouble with all these
dress rehearsals is that
the zipper
is always getting stuck.

AFTER THE QUARREL

When we come up
from our own dregs
we breathe and taste again.
We are clean, clean—
all parts of us taste good.
We sample each other
like new lovers
and the scars lie
in silent ridges
beneath our skin.

THE RUNNER WONDERS

Through the woods the fields,
enmeshed in the machinery of my breathing,
I move through colored veils:
the scent of flowers hanging,
drifting on green wind.

The fragrance clings to my teeth
as I suck in air;
my mouth is full of the colors
on the wind.

Yet nothing could be more precise
then the ticking of my body.
My breathing downshifts;
the computer in my head
projects my results for each
well measured and metrical mile.
The pain is tabulated and tolerable.

And somewhere far inside,
riding in a small space
at the top of my head,
I dare to ask, "Why?"

The only answer seems to be
in the words of the woods
as they wrap me in green
and a rainbow of wind, and say,
"Never mind, never mind."

STATE MENTAL HOSPITAL, 5 PM, SUMMER

The picnic tables,
empty.
The bright benches,
empty.
It is not the hour for sitting in the sun
or in the shade.

    Wire mesh windows
    force the view
    into patterns.

Empty lawns,
empty sky.
The grass can wait until tomorrow;
the sky does not really ever fall.

    (Note: but we have
            plenty of glue here,
            just in case.)

DOWNHILL

I don't have a home,
and I live there
all the time.

DEAL

You can't control anger,
and you can't control us,
so you say we must be angry.
     (But we are angry
      very angry,
       rhythm of bodies that refuse to rhyme.)

You're afraid of beauty,
and afraid of us,
so you say we must be beautiful.
     (But we are beautiful
      very beautiful,
       embroidered with veins and drunk with time.)

We're logical fallacies,
so give us a dime.

MORNING

Laughter rough as a carthorse
tangles our streets like wrinkles in velvet.
Fog slides down our faces and the walls.
Purses and primitives rehearse a casual laugh;
warm up a shrugging tone, or turn, or both,
One eye on the weather.
The Flower-Man who never smiles
coaxes and calms his roses, under his breath,
while the city opens
its drowsy sun
and the husk of our hands sheds another skin.

SUMMER MURDER

You paced naked in my room like another cage,
pulling your beard and giving me lectures on art,
dunking my poems in turpentine,
exasperated, and hungry with your hands.
You look like a lost trombone
and have short tufts of hair in your ears.
I meant to use you delicately for that social convenience:
a broken heart.
But my nerve broke instead
and I think you'd prefer to break my back.
Which of us has enough pride
to leave first in the morning?
                        For we are, at length
                            only another reason to lose sleep.

ANALYSIS

I've been tired lately.
It's not any one thing.
I used to catch a bus to work;
now I stand at the bus stop for several hours
and finally end up walking.
I'm never late, even so.
I like my work
and I do it well.
(If you're ever passing through, come on down.
We have several interesting prospects at the moment.)
Those are nice inkblots.
I've always wondered who makes them.

It isn't the flu,
and it isn't a man.
I've been bored and existential in my time
and it isn't either of those.

Something is beginning.
You know the sort of bright-colored fantasies that everyone
expects
to happen in a little while?
Yes, that's your job.
But mine are starting.
Really.
Like trumpets from a long way off
and I'm tired already.
I don't want them anymore but it's too late to stop them.
I gave them up long ago the way people do.
No, I can't be specific.
I've been comfortable lately
and I don't have room for them.
All those promises coming home to roost.

Well, I've been tired,
   and they never get tired,
   and I won't be shamed before them.
Blind miracles on wild horses,
and me with my reading glasses.
Yes, I exaggerate. No, I won't come back.

THERMODYNAMICS II

Necessary to the calculation
of the living process—the energy
available to push the engines of
our selves;
the fuel we need so we can blaze up once
or twice between the night and night—
I say,
necessary to the calculation
is a wee, small, tidy factor that
laughs the limit to us:
entropy.

It stands inside the furnace of the farthest star—
perhaps it is the ash of ash of ash—
and with unerring hands, it
turns the
damper
down.

LOVE POEM TO THE EARTH

I feed off you.
I breathe from you.
You keep me right-side-up.
But I know something
you don't know.

Someday you'll die.
You old heartbreaker,
someday you'll die.
And if I'm lucky,
when it happens . . .
I'll be everywhere.

And off we'll go together,
married and apart at last,
atom in atom,
honeymooning
through the universe,
taking our time
our time
our time
our time.
We'll visit the whole family—
piece by piece and
dust by dust.

They say that you're too old for me
(and way too big).
They'll see.
You'll smash up small as me.
Your rivers and my rivers,
your mountains and mine,
nerves intertwined.

You cold lover—
we'll hop it to the very edge
and find
no edge at all,
just more of the same,
the same,
the same,
when we're the same,
the same,
the same.

I'll wait for you,
you fickle giver . . .
if the waiting
lasts forever.

going into the office where the unknown dental surgeon keeps me waiting two boys one joker faced and the other curly blunt and upturned talk about a traffic accident. heroic survival. the people are hurled again and again losing their teeth and then their skulls, each time more horrible. but the people reappear they come again, happy they pick up their skatekeys and their bicycles, as yet they do not understand, moving close to one another their heads touching. a horse-shoe shaped bowl with striped mouths kissing the water, enclosed behind wooden edges. the fish come up out of the sea and into the room to talk dragging their guts and fish knives. earlier in my life it was my baby teeth, my grand-mother said "Honor's teeth don't stick out like the picture." it was the end of my childhood security. My father would not pay for the braces the first time. Then when they would not work I went back again, fish have no teeth they are soft and passive their mouths are spongy additions to unresisting water. I am here again. There is no improvement that will satisfy them. I am not the incinerator to burn myself away at will, I cannot despise myself . . . my cousin Lee "you have a mouth like an old person you will need braces to push out your lower lip." does she sleep with her thumb in her mouth? let's see Honor those wire things they put on their children to keep them from sucking their thumbs. Dentists believe no reports. They thought the child guilty of destroying his own mouth. . . . my friend sue at ten with the behavior of a very old lady treating the braces like an ashamed person treats her sexuality. "the retainer is shaped like a crab." "don't bite your tongue." a generation of over-eager dentists straighten teeth too far back into the head, women's mouths age more readily. When they put them on we went to Shreveport, all hedges and white self-important houses to see a redhaired doctor. Felman? After this is over said my father I will buy you a steak. I did not see it. I tried to eat and cried. My father thought it was comical. that horrible vulnerability. I seem inferior to the kids with mouths already built. John Battenberg just did a sclupture a cast of slender thighs and belly and then grafted into the belly an upper palate and part of a protrusive awkward upperlip John cast from a spiritual redhead. inside another set of teeth. the whole thing in black wax. I can't look at it objectively. since the braces did not work the first time I went into my father's office to tell him that I have to have them again and he screamed at me in front of all the people. . . . I had no discretion telling him this in front of the office. Slowly he began to hate me. An old thing like a man hating his wife's expensive fight against age. never enough money to protect me. I caught him looking at me from the corner of his eyes; I did not care, I hardened. Finally my teeth were capped. My astral body does not have teeth, I have seen it a diaphanous blue mass with a suspicious blackness at the mouth and points for teeth. In the middle of the capping Jim Gilbon, Lauren's partner came in to talk eyes soft as a cat's attracted to the pain. While I recovered he told me about earthquakes in the Philippines; It took four hours. Everything turned blue and went far away from me. . . . my cousin and my aunt and my uncle hit a cow on the way to Meeker. There.are a lot of very poor farmers in Louisiana. The cattle consequently are not required by law to be fenced in. They graze on public land. . . . without that the farmers would die. the cow went halfway through the windshield and my cousin lost all of his front teeth. For a long time he would do nothing about it. there was a piece of destroyed flesh on his upper lip. Then slowly he began to wear the bridge and this flesh was cut away. I still have a deep scar. I dreamed last night that someone had cancer of the mouth and they had to cut his lips off, but they planned to grow his mustache out to hide it. A dream of elevators and ineffective plans. we were going to a new place to live. I went to have the cap changed. I wanted to do something and it did not occur to me to do this. I was badly frightened and Collin put me into a room with rattling blinds. slowly reality became gray and faded away. I saw myself from multiple directions, inside a world of gray saxophones and neon effervescence. objects lit like flames and appeared to me more than once. sometimes they, half there, blotting out my vision, slowly subsided. . . .

Lee said I had an inadequate mouth which he then tried to make adequate by stuffing a piece of cotton in the underlip (they do that for corpses.) made my mouth a little fuller but it ripped the gum tissue from the sides of the gums. there were inflammations, my whole mouth had to be painfully rearranged.

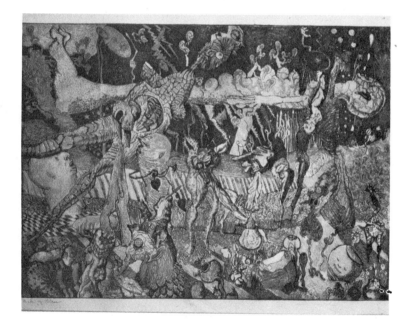

MAXIMS

a field of rationalizations over
a network of black poppies that
recede further and further from
vision. . . . nothing is left and the
actors are going home from the
gymnasium, the place they
lingered in their youth
awaiting journeys.

as a person of poverty he
anticipated castration at the
outset and his melancholy had
a depth of tone even in youth
that caused him the greatest social
frustration.

the feeling that we were left
seemed to follow us destroying
our sense of status, but
without any content either
forgotten rhythms that one
feels an impulse to follow.

every person should open his
mouth and there should be
great arias that come from him
said my friend to the social problem.

contact is not possible without
power, the tiger with no teeth
has no force   the first law
of nature. . . .

sight is the last facility that man
learns and the last subtlety he is interested
in apart from counterfactual thought.

life ends when passion ends. . . .

black poppies that are felt underlying
and shading the voices that we pass
which if we reach for we are severely punished. . . .

come away death. . . . is it death that comes away
or ourselves, or only time that comes away
licking its jaws. . . .

black sorrows fade, even as organic forms
part of the loss that is only a petal is
remembered. . . .

all of the used adjusted people on the streets
remember being beautiful. . . .

a person who still has eros is an object of envy.

competition is participation in the death of
responsiveness. . . . that there must be a standard
evidence in the fear of shame.

your childhood is leaving you.

your past experiences no sadness in your departure.
violent meaningful incidents forget your name.

decay is a component that is not necessary to growth
but is evidence of divine cruelty. . . .

Cruelty is evidence that god retains a certain fatigued
evil interest in our whereabouts. . . .

TARANTELLA

Teller of tales sat on a beehive
his possums could no longer sleep:

    Raven pulled First Man
    from the belly of Salmon

    Bear laid down
    from his dreams fell Snow

    Ocean foamed and
    spit out Forest

Sanddunes rose from
skin shed by Sky
music moves below water
to the drums of our fathers
flutes baked by our mothers
the scales of grandparents,
octaves bleeding in sleep
I've been bitten
and will dance 'till the singing's over
the dance of the deer running from panther
you hold me by my bracelets
they burn & become smoke
my trail is the bird crossing water.

TO, FROM, FOR AND ABOUT DETROIT

for Faye Kicknosway

the child
with her wounded knee
limps across an empty lot
these are tears
we've all seen
flames of cities
in rusted beer cans
that slash like stilettos
able to chop down trees.
At night the metal pin in my knee
sends messages in code
which are mistaken for
summer locust in a tree
I smell the child
who's grown older than me
a dwarf with white hair
hobbles out of the candy store
these lights—
pencils which hurt like knives
wine in a park
where a pawn is queened.
a city of women of iron & salt
who walk with invisible weapons
their menstrual flow is molten metal
in bed they burn & hiss.
a woman leans from the window
her hair is loose—her breasts drip
she bends & moans like a willow
my knee transmits gray
it's my grandfather
the checker-board
on the picnic table
is covered with ants

the child drags her wounded knee
she
is the dust
that falls from my fingers.

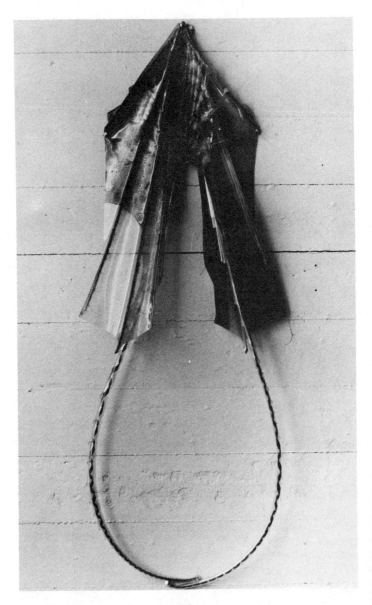

A LOVE POEM

You can only go down so far
before becoming hard & erect.
It's this root I'm after
to know its shape
how it plunges
what holds it firm
to feel hair
against bone
to feel length
compelled to action.

DEBUTANTE

The woman in white lies on the lawn
her grass-stained skirt rolled past her knees.
She has a cucumber for a lover
He does it the way she likes—
incestuously clean.
Brother captures it on Polaroid
Father's sperm smears on the windowpane.
Her hair comes loose,
ringlets straighten in damp grass
she's stuffing fistfuls of tulips
in her mouth—tongue coating with pollen.
It's her sister's turn next
waiting primly in the shade
while mother brings out tea.

UNTITLED

we lived next to the tank field
the water tank stood in the center
like some huge adolescent gland
each summer we cleared enough weeds
to form a baseball diamond
the older boys threw stones at my legs.

while necking on a ferris wheel
—i looked down
to see the tank like an eye
on the roof of my mother's house
its shape haunted my wet dreams.

one summer they threw me to the ground
pulled down my pants to see
if Jews were built different
my sounds were the gasps of fish
collapsing
the grass scratched
my underwear was oversized—blue
the tank was laughing.

MISSION STREET BUS

Spastic man
I love you
I want to take you
away from here
home with me
where I will gently take
your shirt from your waving arms
pull your pants off your wobbly legs
kiss your shaking spit flecked lips
I love you
I saw you looking at my thighs
your head twitching
You are employed   I can tell
from the lunch pail
that clatters on your knees
at the next stop
I will get off
I will make no sign to you
but you must follow
as best you can.

THE ORGY

It was your idea to come
that's for sure
I would never have recommended
an orgy
you just want the chance to
show off your big cock
which you think is not
sufficiently appreciated
no one woman alone could
possibly do that
so here I am with a
dentist from San Jose
unzipping my dress and
saying, "Honey, what's
the matter, don't you
want to?" while a whole
pile of people are squirming
over in the corner
sucking and poking at each other
with beatific looks on their faces
when you can see their faces
"You don't have to do anything
you don't want to do," the dentist
says, suddenly explanatory,
"that's what's so beautiful,
anything is cool" and he walks away
after a brunette with dusky pink nipples
and perfectly straight hair pointing
to the dimples on her ass
and where are you my love?
I thought we agreed
if it was too bad
too terrible

I could give you a signal and
you'd come running, well,
where are you?
Should I start searching
the piles of people?
I'm sure some part of you is stuck
in somebody at this very moment
somebody has their hand around my ankle
I'm glad I shaved my legs
there are so many things to do to get
ready for an orgy
a lot of people here
look like porpoises
they have smooth humps of behinds
and faces that are always surfacing
I don't see anybody who is my type
of course, you are my type
but where are you? remember
we agreed?
Do you notice a great difference
in women
I mean, once you are inside them
couldn't it just as well be me
or couldn't you pretend it was me?

WELCOME HOME FROM VIETNAM

His woman knows
he is a war older.
Fear pommels his eyes
when she begs
him to undress.
He has been hiding
under his clothes.
Her fingers have searched.
Now,

Her eyes trace his age
on the stump of his arm.
His groin hardens
with shadows.
At her touch
the medals pinned on his knees
rust with sweat.

He is a shelter
missing a corner.
She must brace him
with her thighs.
When they reach
for the light,
his legs patched
with newspaper
begin to mend.

LIVING WHERE YOU ARE

When I stop at home
I see the windows
have rusted shut

The sprouts
under the towel
are deteriorating

No one is here
to water each procedure or
check the health
of our inventions

I report that
I am still attracted
to small dark men

They sit impatiently
on the chair
in my pelvis

I report however
that I am moving
slower and slower
my blood taking the
consistency of cereal

I have collected all
this evidence
into a sentence

I am dying of you

TONIGHT

the rain is falling
through the gauze air

I will split my brain
and let it clean out
I will look for a doctor
and tell him it's
living that does it
it's waking up
on another side of sleep

there is no one
out here but a dog
following me
he slowly lifts his leg
in a dance

star dog pale yellow
this is no way to
spend the night
wandering around
with my heart
too close to the skin
my sex opening
and closing like an eye

where are you now?
who I want to hold close
warm in the cloth
of your legs

there is only this dog
his eyes gleaming
like metal instruments
a star dog
who talks in his sleep

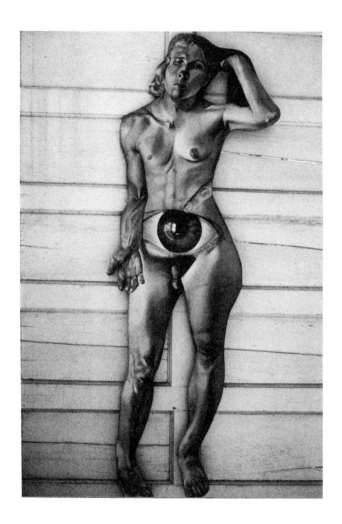

DANCE MAD

Under a hat of sky
I shake the snakes out.
My good eye is happy.

I promise that what is visible
will glisten,
I promise the music of
my astrology.

Tonight, as always,
it is with difficulty
I open a handbook of death.
It suggests only that I
keep moving that I
promise anything.

I do. I've said it before.
I carry its weight
like snake wings
but drop it now
next to my coat.

Tonight I am forgetting everything.
My feet and hands
have their own lives.
My hair falls about my waist
and stings me.
I will dance clapping
until my fingers bruise.

COPY CLERK — NORTH AMERICAN AVIATION

Her birdcage bones
ridge through the flesh
Her hand's a slow exhausted curve
She wasn't made for this—
seven children
and no man
She stares distracted out of her job
stares from round
bewildered eyes
What a surprise!
Seven children and no man
Her mind opens back on a blue sky
she visited once
and wants to return to
forever
At home the babies wait
to climb her sides
She wasn't made for this
growl of machines   and
a boss who makes her cry,
those seven humans who
came from her like Christmas gifts
and now suck the marrow of her bones
They leave her like chimes
in the wind
hollow, languidly moving
a weak tinkle
in the blue sky.

THREE NIGHTS ON HOFFMAN STREET

A madwoman sits on the roof
I hear her at night
when the wires sing in the walls
her thoughts fall like confetti into the rooms
                              of the house
or like flakes of fire
or like snow, drifting down
A mad witch sits on the peak of the roof
I know her by her snowfall
that sears my thighs
my eyelids
Oh witch, I call
      but not loud enough
      in the snow silence
      —come down into the rooms
where your thoughts burn
Come into your mind.

UNTITLED

So we were reading poems
About people dying
   And of course
I thought of you.
These poems
   Were
Descriptions
Of the Death Scene
And so I tried
To put you back
Up on your bike
Life in your legs
Hope in the form
   of an index card message
   in your jacket
I tried to put
You back up there
And let you go . . .

UNTITLED

Provincetown
The night
I glided through the streets
Arms like liquid wings
To mail a postcard home
—Gail and I are happy
on private stock New England Beer
And have no place to sleep—

Medusa MEDUSA Medusa MEDUSA Medusa MEDUSA

'You know how It rained in January, and they were just
full of water, and then It froze, and some of them just
burst open, and mostly all their bark fell off, and of
course the leaves are all over the ground. The eucalyptus
trees are dead. I actually didn't know then, when I, in
a particular thought, want it to be nice to back there
for another little go, but then I myself met nature, then,
as now, and layed on the ground last year when there hadn't
been a frost like that since before anyone planted the
trees, and my smile was just a crooked stick too, and
I actually thought when I went there, and took off my
clothes, and layed on the ground this year when the water
was seeping, actually rising up through the leaves when
you pressed. I thought for a while we could just try it
standing up, and I took off all my own clothes, and layed
them aside, and layed in the seeping leaves, and pulled
him down on me, I didn't know that all the roots weren't
drinking, and the water was actually coming up, and this
was on top of a mountain, and I layed down for him on the
ground, and it was feeling all cool, and I spread my legs,
and made my knees a cradle so that only the tips of his
boots and the sides of his hands touched any of the ground
I tipped my hips up so that not even his balls should
dredge the ground, and I was not afraid of one small bug,
though I saw several before, falling on the ground,
and we rocked and I moaned much, and this tricked him
though I lay in the world and was just on it also, and he,

and the sky, and his face looked like he hated about to crash!
And then he sort of slid down to the end of the cradle, so
that his knees did touch the ground and his face, a part of
his true head, lay just below my breasts, and I brought my
arms up around his head, so that my breasts and arms pressed
this particular man's head in a circle, and I felt, over my
heart, that I could let him know I feel my body, as it is,
surround his head, to surround is alright, and even good to
receive, but I guess the breeze just went up over the
top of his pants that were bunched, and actually hobbling
him. Wind went right up his leg hairs and smooth back
and suddenly he was not covered. Suddenly he got up, and
for a while I just displayed and displayed my cradle, for
what it was with its surprisingly suddenly present on a
pink surface with all its hunger, though it just be one of
the doors. He made as he rared up to get up a tube with
his two hands curled, and pretended to take my picture thus,
and I got up and felt sick because Fuck the World! and my
instinct to complain. Clearly we walked away in shame
after brushing as best we could all the wet dead leaves,
and the sticky bits of last year's decayed leaves from
my back and buttox and everything in my hair too for
my head had writhed.'

TWO GRIEFS BEFORE A DEATH

Anyway, the men wait for typical Italian lasagne and
argue somehow to convince their death better. I do cry
this time, I'm mad. Go in the bathroom! Look in the
mirror to stretch out the grief muzzle. Mouth to tear
and eyes to pop. Don't go. God! Go to the window.
Put my eyes in sky over pretty twilight ice blue with about
two drops of black few natural stars twink some towers
some windows not everybody is home not everybody turns
their light on all the time.

The men are going to eat dinner in spite of the death,
which is a death of one of them either or any one of them
a man is all but dead. They are a cell in my living
room still alive. Bitter. Will eat eat anyway.

Anyway, in the bathroom my arm goes out the window on the
side of the house in the city that makes it seem on the
upper level of a forest. Out the window my arm is very
like a snake. Its hand tears off two ivy leaves from the
giant ivy with my fallen hair stuck all over it for the
birds and to listen. Chew it very bitter and some fern and
some lilac leaf and some coleus and some begonia, fibrous,
and the furry piggy back. CHEW! Hold it, don't gag . . .
Spit into hand, spread the green mash all over the medicine
mirror and the vanity mirror diagonally cracked and on my
own chest too. My arms shout high "I have the power in my
body."

Back in to make herb bread with a straight face. They help
me bring the dinner to the table. I ate with the men and
just for myself I poured the wine down on my breasts three
times through my dress and before I went to sleep I wiped
all the stuff off the mirrors. I laughed at my dinner

looking at it on the fork, I slopped some down on the floor and added to its velocity.

Inside I said I have power through the kitchen wall. My teeth believe it. I call your name. Friend, in the morning my arms wilted. They sit at the dinner board and watch your shadow fall which makes them gruff.

Moose in Mexico and little local deer

stuck in the walls

could their wired rotting legs

be jangling in the walls

do their butts mozery away in the sanitary room

dark-adobe-walls-on-the-way-to-break-my-sack
thats right the streets a cloud
Rusty Service station, one pump

barely room to turn the car in the cactus

so hot out so cold inside me

puke in the cool tin brown unflushable

on about a cup a clean water

thought even an aspirin is bad Yes Yes

can't speak

Look at that fan

this is a cave do you perhaps love me

don't talk only yes yes

no one said you or I or anyone could talk yes yes

everybody's girl, grammas nailpolish & lipstick post

she's so tiny her shoes fit. Dust and board streets . . .

Well . . . it seems to stop her. Harry True Man. Show *you* some lists. Well we all know they won't do. Grampa's September deers. One mounted over his bed. Used to nap in there alone. Rotting. Hardnosed. Touched it. Glass eyes. I saw a deer hang upside down in a garage. It was pink with membrane over it and deer heads and moose heads here in Sunny Meheeco obstetrics.

ANNIE OAKLEY HAD GUNS, HAD BUNS, HAD FEAR AND SHOT WEST

LESSONS

We don't escape any lessons
learned   lived   through
pores living in
the growing of
the child   we were

We bear these lessons through
each day   dark   or   light
they mold our moves
we are the clay of their proof.
And sit and cry inside
to find ourselves
a bag of Past
to reach once more
what we thought was
New

THE DIFFERENCE

It involves a simplicity,
the difference between men and women.
Women render from complexity
A simpler face.
For that, men think her simplistic.
But she is not.

It's a matter of living:
living equals people.
That is what you will find
when a woman draws the lines.

But do not think it stops there.
The lines are only possible
in the round
that holds them, buoying,
like a mother holds a child.

RUNNING SCARED

Dear Husband,

Your letters are here;
I pull the white turkey-meat pieces
out of their envelopes.
There is the smell of your stove,
your house,
I am afraid of them.
It is not *these* words that I want,
but still, I do not let the aromas escape.

To celebrate the anniversary
of our relationship,
I am giving you
a life-sized replica of myself,
and have stuffed the private parts
with *Dear Abby* columns
and old grocery sacks;
      Or should I give it to my Father?
That Father, who never spoke—
always tired,
tired of commuting
those 60 miles a day
to the slaughter house
on the Columbia River slough:
But later, when Mother filled out
my ''Family History''

for the Portland State College Health Facility,
she told them
that you thought I was crazy.
But then, Daddy, you had talked to her
and told her so.

And, Husband,
in my half-sleep
I am not sure which one of you
is speaking.
The ring of your axe
the wail of your chain saw,
they do not answer my questions.
Who is who?
Who is who.
Where are you, Daddy?
I have looked for you in everyone.
And I dream that I am falling
through the rafters of your house
leaving
my stomach an empty bowl
where the terror in me hides:
I feed it chocolates,
I feed it often,
but it never goes away
and I am sick from the smell of it.

Husband,
I have clung to you
sucking
with hysterical hunger.
Now the energy is dry
and I am limp and knowing
that I've never loved any man at all . . .
Yet this force that binds *us*
is stronger than the moon;
you have the power to diminish me

like acid
and I have been waiting for you
to leave me for years:
    You can't understand my poems
    my pants are too tight,
    you say my pet moths are dirty
    and carry infections,
    but all the same
    they need me.
    I spend my time looking
    for things that I think I have
    and there is nothing that I do that is right.

Those Lovers whom I laid against
on the warm rocks of the Clackamas River
when I was seventeen. . . . Where have they gone?
I have lost the girl who came from that river,
and no stone marks her death sleep—
Now, in backwashes and sewers
the fish run from me like rats;
I stand thigh deep and ridiculous in water
Wondering, if I should stay or leave.

But, Daddy, this man and I,
We have chopped cords of wood;
Teaching me
that it's not the strength of the blow
but the speed of the axe
that splits the wood in half.
But there is a fog between us,
Him and I,
The walls are black from it.
Do not think it will go away;
I have been born into it.
Where are you, Daddy?
Bats are biting the first stars resentfully,
and the face of the moon terrifies me,

and I am afraid of what I am.
Daddy, you never wrote me letters
So I've found someone else to need.
But I wonder how many it will take
before I won't want you anymore. . . .
        And in my half-sleep
        I am not sure
        which one of you
        is speaking.

POEM FOR A STRANGER

Thin,
long mustard weed;
When I was ten
I rolled in fields of it.
The hot taste of the flower
on my tongue.
Now, I want to bite down
to the stalk
and eat acres of you:

I had watched him for weeks,
he remembered lines of my poems,
but didn't remember my name.
There was the smell of rain
on concrete streets,
the pink of plum flowers.
I had forgotten the way
that the leaves of Acacias
close up at night,
their yellow aroma
fills by bedroom;
I am crazy
from the smell of it.
I lay awake
feeling my way back
to the smoke-blue arms
of wild lilac trees.

He said he became a gardener
because plants
never put him down.
There is only that *one* night
we spent together;

Speaking more of your life
to me
than the man
I've lived with for 3 ½ years . . .

Stranger,
My hair blows like flax,
I am the grass;
I am obsessed with you.
But my bones itch
there is something wrong,
I smell it
on my fingers.
I am wound like a clock,
I tick away.
The sun has gone down
without me,
Night birds in the Cypress
pant like dogs, knowing
that all I have of you
is a poem.

THE WOMAN, AFTER FOUR YEARS OF
LIBERATION, ADDRESSES HIM:
HER SISTERS HEAR HER

YES, AS ALL the men, the entire media, and many women hoped, we have moved beyond anger. It's called the acquisition of wisdom, but it's not like the journey to Ixtlan, the quest of the Holy Grail, the holy wars, the initiation into sex, the scientific pursuit, the rites of passage, or any other of those ceremonies so loved by male fantasy. Small episodes of insight, such as the abuse by one's spouse after one has said, "Hear me; I don't *want* to be ordered around," spread quietly into a thin and translucent stain. No, *he's* not coloring my life red; I used to be blue, but that was adolescence; this is maturity and the civilized horror our most elegant, symbolic dreams always knew it to be. I dreamed of huge waters outside fragile window panes encased in weathered wood; then came the tidal wave, but we held on to the deck and were not washed overboard. The scene moves; we are on the ship, sailing over a basin of water ultimately clear—so clear we see deep below us Elizabethan rowboats, with the couples (man and woman, daunsing although sitting still), fully dressed, with subtle postures of calm. *We* are alive, I realize; unlike them, *we* have survived the tidal wave, that huge anger. The water turns into stairs going downward, moving toward spacious lawns; down these steps moves the utmost in funeral splendor—but the expensive cars leave mud on the carpeted steps. I realize: they are dead, we must be dead;

this is style, if not understanding. Don Juan calls it the loss of personal history; no sorcerer has to tell *me*, why do all the men think they have to tell *us*, *we* had no personal history anyway—"I hope your life has a good day today," he sneers as he leaves, "I get so tired of 'your life,' 'your life.'" No, *I* don't get tired of it; the stain is spreading; the color will heighten my camouflage; I will live in the house of mine enemy and shall do as I please; I am invisible now, no anger indicates my outline; there will be nothing for you to shoot at, and no one will answer back; some services will cease, but others will continue. This resembles the former state; having cast out thirty-three devils, many more have re-entered. Guilt never left anyway, so I was not surprised to see it among these. THIS IS: knowledge with wonder, surprise at the familiar, the miracle of adventure within the four walls of his house. Such excess of wisdom, and within so short a time, too. I learned so much the past four years that I let drop great armfuls, extra ideas, histories, emotions; I was still moving, I couldn't carry it all, and besides, there was more where those came from; women's abundances were my security. Now I've stopped moving, I sit in a sunlight soaked with color, and all my knowledges come home—home is where he is, he picked up pieces of what I dropped and adds them to his conversation, where he talks about my ideas and tells others he doesn't believe I really mean them, they are another of my excesses, and my childhood wasn't really that bad anyway. *Yes it was,* my love; so is my womanhood; I have come, as they say, full circle, I have moved beyond anger, but I'm not dropping any hints any more, so I can't tell you what it's like; hush now, as we say to children; peace, as we tell adults; love, as we sign letters to strangers; silence in the wonder of the world.

LATER, TO JEAN-PIERRE

Maintenant que tout c'est fini,
that the Nanciens talk no more of the light on my nipples,
and even the U.S. Army has left France

now let my speaking love you.

When I lay down, you breathed flowers on me like a lion
and I came like a buttercup
    while the moon watched
    and the stars said yes.
My child fingers had reached for you
    and my breasts grew toward you.
If it rained, the sun rose with your cock and whirled
    madly in the heaven of my thighs.
What every mother feared, you did like roses in haystacks
    on green glass water

and when you left, the sun flowed down my legs.

AN EXPRESSION

anger
is killing
my face.
it squints all day
despite cool remarks
it thinks the sun
is after it.
it thinks the whole
fucking world
is after it!
building armies
above the brow

anger
is killing
my face.
it squints all day
despite cool remarks
it thinks the sun
is after it.
it thinks the whole
fucking world
is after it!
building armies
above the brow
just in case.

meanwhile, no one
notices; even suspects
go about private
maneuvers.
one day,
wrinkles will tell
stories like old soldiers
when my lips have nothing
left to say,
pain will lean forward
and speak
for itself.

THE PROCESS OF DISSOLUTION

my husband held me
responsible for his failures.
when he scolded me
he had my father
written all over his face.
our marriage ended
as my childhood
continued; the men in my life
still try teaching me lessons,
and i have not ceased entirely
from kicking myself hard
to please them: damn you
daddy. damn your redundant
face.

HER ROOMS

these are her rooms,
her way of bringing you
into them, serving
a patchwork quilt, mozart
camomile tea.
she is delighted
you came.
she was alone (lonely)
before you
so she opens up
drawers, shows you
pictures, feeds
you lines.
later, she will boot
you out and spill
tears all over the quilt
like ice cubes,
like the rooms
she opens up to you
a quick tour, a shutter.

KAISER HOSPITAL TRILOGY: THREE WOMEN
AT THE MERCY OF UNKNOWN GODS

I

a woman is slicing meat;
her thumb interrupts the chore.
wrapped in paper towels
she is driven to the emergency
door, where a 3 x 5 index
card greets her: "The emergency
room has been moved."
a trail of blood leads her across
the street, around a corner,
thru a corridor and into the laps
of doctors sipping coffee.
"We'll be with you in a moment,"
they say to the thumb, finishing
a private joke before putting
the needle thru her carelessness.

II

a second woman arrives open
flipped thru doors her body
concentrates on breathing life
between her thighs, works at
controlling pain, pushing
a labor of love.
they strap her to the table,
the slab they've known for an hour
and shoot her up with sleep.
her gift is lifted smoothly
from the ditch and a steady
scissors comes down to cut
the cord; a new born child
swiftly wrapped and sealed away
from germs while the mother dreams
of giving birth.

III

a third woman receives foreign
signals thru her breast.
"a harmless cyst," the doctor
smiles. "you are a worry wart,
my dear." weeks later, the harmless
cyst is twice its size and bleeds
for an incision. the woman changes
color as rage pounds her chest.
unalarmed, the doctor concedes
to cut her open; the malignancy
flows out howling and will not stop.
two months later, the woman of 25
dies quietly at home; her lover
cradles her last bits of life
in his arms and dreams of mercy
from unknown gods.

NOT QUITE MAKING IT

today, you came upstairs breaking
the news of al's death
bent over your black coffee
mourning the absence
or is it the presence we fall
apart about?
making sounds and rattling
the daily newspaper i'm struck
dumb by such hard
cold facts. some people will
say he was wonderful others
didn't know him and what difference
does it make in the end
whether we mention he was 34
married but not exactly
happy, did it to himself in
washington d.c. wasn't there
very long.
it's far, far away
death is
and we sit breaking
our brains
trying to rub up against
it before
we go on
living.

POSTAGE DUE

Teaching physics back in North Dakota, my brother never
                                                    writes,
Only a card at Christmastime, with snow
That really twinkles as it bites in
Through the Berkeley marijuana sun. And all my cosmic
Poems trail off, like stumblebums and stiffs
Losing touch with prairie clotheslines in the blizzard . . .
Pure glare of Reason! It even scares

The teenage queers
Under the Shorts Beach pier. It freezes half my head
Cabbage as the moon, in lilac drag
I put on just to make my brother mad
Enough to dive and save me. And he has:
Although the continent
Stretches between us, laid waste by Daddy's
Ham-fisted Science and Mama's voodoo Art,

Somehow I've hauled myself across
The desert or boiling ocean of their marriage bed,
To solid ground.
Only to find him standing there before me — my stupid
                                            little brother —

Holding the darkness and the crud together,
With streetlamps lighting sidewalks through small towns
Of the wild universe;
No words I know
Make home.

THE FAULT

too much energy she tried to show with
her hands moving outward

how it smothered
how one's joy could create fear like yeast in the shy person

how the jingle of keys makes someone important

I was circling this
sniffing what i hadn't paid attention to other times

that his hairs were all yellow gold
wiring out of a center of energy &
I felt myself in love with him watching his tongue run over
                                                    his lips
and remembered Fredericka
                        always keeping the tube of
                        vaseline in her purse
always gliding it over her mouth should there be someone
                                                    to kiss

and thought how I liked space and long unending lines,
                        how my life was that way
without visible connections or obvious explanations

                                        how I was glad
I'd washed my hair

WHAT YOU NEED

What you need is
a compliment to plump you up

tired ass down flat to blue chair
                              (supposed to be a touch of
                                             brightness)
yes
your mind jumped at *that* when she said how are you
and you tried not to tell

but to be a sample and a dimple
and finding the proper response to goodness   to a really
                                             kind question

And then he handed it to you
the quick observation that you looked beautiful   and oh
your heart let go a spurt
                        a little thin skin cracked and loos-
                                                       ened

propelled yourself up the hill and into the ladies & gents
                                             and cookies
tasting of wallpaper paste . . . your ideal in her perfect suit
                                             went by
and glad you'd sewn the button on at the last

You are alone but don't listen

All of literature rains down lots of commas

And even feel fine most evenings   sliding into the flowered
                                             sheets
so relieved to have your spreading to all corners two could

fit in easily

Bones fall gently towards the floor   you sleep with regular
breathing

It's the unexplained wakings and where they leave you

In a clearing
with someone who loved you
alive in the dark

You are brave   but you need to be touched

THE STRANGER

"It is yourself you fall in love with" when the mysterious
                                       stranger appears
with his solution of soft drinks.

You like to think about Pepsi and RC Cola and those sweaty
                                       Dr. Peppers
in the lower grades
                 and the green play yards not yet all
                                       asphalt.
And then He comes.
Like a jungle jim of peculiar but apprehensive right angles
and you know in your heart you can climb him.

It is the shining and the light you can see flowing amidst
                                      the cubes
and he is your *self*
                 or that steely part of you that seeks
                                  definition
                 and wants to sturdy yourself
as an alloy of metals creates an argument of strength.

The "little girl" games you loved,
the giant popcorns in cardboard cartons greasy with fake
                                      butter,
the bigger-than-life bodies that awaited your feelings'
                                    membrane—
all tell you
                 you must set aside the metallic thrust of sadness.
It is a kind of sobbing that gets started and doesn't want to
                                      stop.
You would wish to curl up inside its waters,
float through the moist black-and-white romances
                 and have your solitude in luxuri-
                                ous technicolor,

thinking you are moving,
                        while from out here we can see
                                    that you may be stuck
in the compromise of whole-heartedness,
when on the other side of this childhood a flag is waiting
                                    with its code
locked into two existing colors and the key is in your
                                    feelings
which are about to bear fruit in those clear reds and
                                    yellows.

"Coming at an end the lovers"
could be a beginning for each other's
new expansiveness

They are exhausted, they think,
like two hikers who kept seeing the final ascent

And come from other romantic attachments
still coiled with rope
or the long good-bye

To the new each other
they do not disguise

Talk is possible   it has endings
provides a meadow or
                            an unfolding of hills
for the love
of no finality

For unexpectedly
they are two persons   Shyly
new   she coils inside his covering
like fruit   she feels small but appropriate
for the next hike
                    as tho supplies for long distances
could be guessed at accurately

He changes shape   at ease in the room
with her   His shape is right

His questions pull her out of the middle
of the coil of rope

so that finding the end she may understand
where it rested
and that she might step out of its circling
to the bare floor

But, you will say, the lovers
had loved others   That some part of each
would remain in that coil   Yes
but they are two persons
two bodies waiting to expand into
the inexhaustible
open

THE EARLIEST DAYS

I lived under the house for quite a few years.
The ocean came as far as the third step of the front porch,
But no farther. I would crawl up to it,
Stick my fingers in the salt water and lick them.
This was how I lived. There were no other sounds.
I read books by flashlight and thought about scarey things.
One book had pictures of an African tribe. Bare breasts.
I stared at them for hours and rubbed dirt on my chest.
Another book talked about "a healthy lawlessness."
It seemed some kind of test. Feet
Became immensely important. That's all you have to go by
When you can't stand up. Wheels are important to most people,
But not to me. I didn't know what "a couple" was.
There was no need to be near you.
One spring, the dirt became soggy, and I wanted a bath.
Do women go home because they need to travel
Or because they want to be part of the bedspread?
I walk up the porch steps, leaving a trail behind, and sit in a chair.
The light makes me sick. The best cure for reflection being sleep,
I dream I am under the porch again, only you are with me,
And you read the book on lawlessness.
Everything is blown away. It settles in a different arrangement.

The portrait is in black and white,
And as in most self-portraits,
The artist is not smiling. Emotion
Is represented by small, quivering lines
Around the stomach area.   .
What makes this self-portrait most uncommon
Is the inclusion of a second figure on the canvas.
He is a doctor named Victor Hugo.
We will not describe this portion of the canvas
At this time, other than to note that the artist
Has represented him with two flat, round heads.
These heads face the viewer,
While the head of the artist is in profile.
The scope of the background can only be compared
To that of the Mona Lisa.
It is late at night. The moon is high.
Through the windshield hundreds of birds can be seen.
The viewer can hear a mosquito
Buzzing around the artist's ears,
And will hear this mosquito every night
For months. He will also look for the man
In the market and zocalo.
Once the viewer realizes that the artist
Is not going to be killed, he will be able to imagine
The amazing progression of this painting.
This self-portrait is the most powerful
Of any to date, including "Earthquake."
It is dated Progresso, Sept. 4, 1973.
When I interviewed the artist,
She pointed out the hard edges and sharp tonal division.
These techniques, she said, were used to recreate the moment
With as much clarity as possible.

ROCK BOTTOM NOURISHMENT

When I was a young girl, I entered the room with authority.
I used my eyes to gain strength.
I possessed my neck.
For instance:
I am a tree with light on my neck.
No bookend can support me.
There is the door; take it if you believe in betrayal.
Thus sayeth the greyhound, the big cat of imagination,
The batterer of speed.

Then the girl realized that when you turn off the motorcycle
You don't travel anywhere,
So she got off and walked.

I have made myself plain.
I've learned to hold myself like a walnut
In my hand, and I've taken the dollar bills off my dress.
I've taken off my dress,
Yet I regret it.
I've made myself timid,
But I'm not like spring.
There's a rock over the mouth of my cave
That makes me more like another season.
Besides, I've been here too long.
My past is accumulating.

I used to splendour
In my frivolity. Oh, procession of energy,
Where have you gone? You have put a shopping list
In my hand. You've left me
Holding my thighs. I no longer want everything,
And I've lost my deadliness.
I catch glimpses of that kid

Diving into the pool with the wind
Around her neck, and though I've been caught
in New York City,
I'll be in the reception hall of changes. It's
In my stomach. I'm shedding my flowers,
And if you think these are the words of a girl
Getting back on the bike, you're right.
I've seen the choices.
It's better to live with your motor running
And best to travel somewhere.

IN ANSWER TO WHAT HE SAID

for peterpaul

i am indeed the lady in the supermarket slapping her kid
suburbanite shopper for meat
owner of a baby blue ford stationwagon to haul it
holder of six major credit cards
whimperer in the bed of a space engineer husband
sado-masochistic voyeur on the patio of dawn
belly-acher washing toilet bowls for eternity
friend-destroyer by way of cuckolding
drinker of straight scotch in the afternoon of salads
knowing my life's running out while i'm peeling potatoes
stuck with fried eggs and ovulation
stuck with the certainty of another 20 years of menstruation
starving to death in the middle of Thanksgiving Dinner
bones creaking under the weight of babies
skin wrinkling in the dry climate of everything sacred to women
face shrinking to the bone it bitterly wants to be

you opened me like a silent rose in a holocaust of your tongue
you peeled me to the shimmering galaxies of cell division
you broke me from the egg into mercies of water
you stripped me into breath by the ringing of bone
you wounded me on the wheel of birthing stars by your hair
you ripped me to my first eyes in the dawn of your fingers

and left me like a bitch with a hole full of children
turned down the stair with my blood on your lip
blasted the future into millions of clocks
took out my eyes so the trees turned to ice
left my fingers as dangerous as guns

i could sit in my tower writing books of glass
i could kill every child i see in the sky
i could tie up the roses into bundles of straw
i could bury the eggs in black pools for judgement

i say stand up and acknowledge my nipples
i say reel into my cries when you can
i say take off your mind like a shirt when you see me
i say look into distances we fill with wings

for i'll weave you a tomb that's as soft as a cradle
i'll brush you with milk that kills and resurrects you
i'll make your bones want to giggle to sleep
i'll take you into eggs that eat up your tears
i'll pull out the fish that had drowned and free you

ALONE, WE DREAM AS GODS

1.
Shivering, cold, I run
Blindly into the city.
The narrow white streets
Fall into shadow, destination.
Hurry: where are the people
Populated with faces
I no longer own?
Anonymous as stone,
A clutter of feet,
I wake
Solid, substantial.

2.
Waking. Another white dream.
In the hospital room someone
Is speaking a language I
Can almost understand.
Obedient, my hands move over
The linens like coarse
White lemons.
Clean and infantile,
What has been taken
From me? Whose body is
This with lemons
And pomegranates,
The neat arrangement of pain.

3.

In the third country of white
She is the ghost of color.
Someone has died. Purple and
Orange no longer exist,
Only the succulent membranes,
The bare translucent skin,
Pierced and backlit
Like ancestral walls.
She tries to remember
What it was she
Forgot. Finally
She drifts in a dimpled
Purity, in a peaceful
Falling.

4.

This is your dream.
We are masked in white.
Our eyes have no pupils.
My breasts are white
Immaculate marble.
I touch you
Frozen, erect. We cannot
Move, locked in the storm
Of our own perfection:
The trapped egg, the sperm.

5.

There is a fifth whiteness
Called   Reality. The brush
Before canvas
The words   scattered
Seeds.
These constellations
Tell us nothing.
To be blank   empty.

I am filling out my life
Line by line.
No matter how I do it
It will all come out
The same.

LADY, SISTER: FOR JANIS JOPLIN

Lady, Sister, it is cold
Out here, there is snow falling, monstrous,
White, and the country beyond the motel's
Walls is thrown back like crumpled
Sheets. Sleep is fixed in our eyes
Like a long parade.

Your voice burns with faces
Of lions; fills the charged air, changing,
Changing, until the moan of the sun in
Your mouth comes
Blinding, ancient raw as bones.
Woman of fur and ostrich,
Strange electric
Hair, change us, change us.

No jagged lullabies. No waking.
Out of the black heavens
One searing constellation: Pain.
It was almost Texas: crashing
in the bitter snow—one steel ray driven
Between the slats of the white motel
Room, where you turned, whirling like a compass,
North, suddenly mortal.

IN DEFENSE OF CIRCUSES

We are the aliens of this world,
doing rope tricks, handling snakes,
allowing you to say, *incredible,
bizarre.* For the small price
of admission, a ticket, you pass
through us, as if we were
attractions, then leave, back
to your homes, your known
predictable lives, where magic
is irrelevant, undesirable.

WEDDING POEM

For Rich and Melanie

Distance does not occur. You carry
my name on your tongue. I bloom.
I would wrap distance around us, marry
its sound to this noon
for we have run out of words.
It is summer. The hill rejoices
in sun; congregations of birds
fill the pines with small voices.
The wind moves in mutual wonder.
This natural world has no reason
to long for endless Spring, nor to be younger
than it is. Here, the fullest season,
on this most lovely of planets, this hill,
we join with rings and flowers. Trace
only the beginnings; what comes will fill
all emptiness. The world invents our face.

With each pain
She screams at God. Though the door
Is shut and nurses try to quiet her
With talk, I hear her howling
For salvation. Another pain
Begins: I grip the bed, feeling
The flesh grow tight, intensely
Mount until I cannot breathe
To cry aloud; an alien head
Locks firm in the bones
And I and the woman in the next
Room are sisters in madness.
The white sweep of the clock
Shortens our breathing; a face
Sealed in a green mask peers
Down at me, looms in my nightmare
Like a rational voice. Doctors,
Midwives of living practice their deep
And hidden art while the women
They fear suffer and hasten
Their death. Oh sister, madness
Becomes us: these Gods are mortal,
We must endure them. Pain
And forgetting: the clock
Brings closer to that hour
When we cheat death
With our bodies.

THE POET INVITES THE MOON FOR SUPPER

Tonight a stranger followed me home.
He wore an overcoat and feathers.
His head was as light as summer.
When I saw how much light he spilled
on the street, I knew he was rich.

He wanted to make me his heir.
I said, no thank you, I have a father.
He wanted to give me the snow to wife.
I said, no thank you, I have a sweetheart.
He wanted to make me immortal.
And I said, no thank you, but when you see
somebody putting me into the mouth
of the earth, don't fret.
I am a song.
Someone is writing me down.
I am disappearing into the ear of a rose.

NIGHT RISING

I gave my small son
  a plastic rose
and then forgot.

But in the night
  suddenly he stood
among us. Not

for the bathroom,
  not for water or light,
but for the rose.

which in the night
  he needed. And I
wanted to ask

where he was going
  that a rose, held
like a wand or a mask

could take him,
  and if other faces
waited in that

room, in the last
  traces of clocks
and mirrors

creaking to sleep,
  crouched like birds
which only the blind

eye of the rose could keep.

BONE POEM

The doctors, white as candles, say,
You will lose your child.
We will find out why.
We will take a photograph of your bones.

It is the seventh month of your life.
It is the month of new lambs and foals in a field.

In the X-ray room, we crouch on an iron table.
Somebody out of sight takes our picture.

In the picture, my spine rises like cinder blocks,
my ribs shine like the keys on a flute,
my bones, scratched as an old record,
have turned to asbestos, sockets and wings.

You are flying out of the picture,
dressed in the skin of a bird,

leaving your bone-house like a shaman.
You have folded your bones like an infant umbrella.

Here we are both skeletons, pure as soap.
Listen, my little shaman, to my heart.
It is a hunter, it beats a drum all day.
  Inside run rivers of blood, outside run rivers of water.
  Inside grow ships of bone, outside grow ships of steel.

The doctor puts on his headdress.
He wears a mirror to catch your soul
which roosts quietly in my ribs.
Thank God I can tell dreaming from dying.

I feel you stretching your wings.
You are flying home.
You are flying home.